THE VIETNAM WAR

THE VIETNAM WAR

DOUGLAS WELSH

BISON

Distributed by
Frederick Fell Publishers Inc.
386 Park Avenue South,
New York, NY 10016.

Published 1984 by
Bison Books Corp.
17 Sherwood Place, Greenwich, CT 06830.
USA.

ISBN 0-8119-0614-0

Printed in Hong Kong

CONTENTS

1 THE VIET MINH'S VICTORY

Of all American wars Vietnam is without doubt the most complex and controversial. Before World War II the affairs of Southeast Asia held little interest for the American people. It became a battlefield which consumed American interest and sent shockwaves of discontent, disorientation and disillusionment through the nation. To best understand the complexity of the Vietnam issues, which America took so lightly in its smug belief in its own right, might and technology, it is necessary to go back to the days of colonialism in Southeast Asia.

Before the era of French Colonialism, Indochina designated a loose grouping of peoples of different cultural backgrounds whose sole common denominator was their conquest by the Chinese Empire. When the French took control of Indochina they proved to be no better masters than the Chinese. As was so often the case, France abused its colonial power. Although there were intermittent revolts in some areas, the people of Indochina lacked a common front which could unite into a formidable force until World War II. Japan, a rapidly growing nation, set out to create an empire worthy of the Japanese ideology through military strength and technology. To accomplish its goal Japan was forced into direct confrontation with the Western world.

In the opening days of World War II Japan not only confronted the United States and European nations that had colonial footholds in Asia but dealt these nations defeats so resounding that many considered the Japanese invincible. To strengthen its position and bind together the loose confederation of Asiatic states under the auspices of the Japanese emperor, Japan began to fan the discontent in Asia with the battle cry 'Asia for the Asians.' This slogan would unite the peoples of Asia and Indochina in an effort to throw off their yoke of Imperialism. More importantly, Japan clearly demonstrated that European armies could be defeated by Asian forces. Although Japan was recognized as being another colonial power, this point was well taken by those who sought the independence of Indochina. The defeat of Japan was not unwelcomed as it opened the way for the peoples of Indochina to become the masters of their own destiny.

However, after World War II the victors were prepared to resume their prewar roles. The French were no exception. As quickly as possible French troops entered Indochina to reestablish their colonial rule, paying little attention to the changed mood and political atmosphere. France only wanted to revive the proof of potency that its colonies represented and failed to recognize that the war had welded many of the people and their leaders into a fine military coalition which had fought well against the Japanese and was ready to continue to fight. The people of Indochina had not fought to throw off the Japanese conquest to then stand idly by while the French returned to burden them once again.

The strongest element of this new movement was the Indochinese Communist Party led by a well-known revolutionary Nguyen Ai Quoc better known as Ho

Chi Minh. He was the driving force behind the political and military organization, the Viet Minh. Ho Chi Minh led his forces well against the Japanese and had gained support not only from his own people but from the United States. American OSS teams supported his war with Japan and for a time the United States considered him the best possible candidate to head a government in Indochina. When the French returned, Ho Chi Minh and his nationalist movement confronted them with major issues of self-determination and independence. France found comfort in the

that maintaining support for his movement would require careful planning and went so far as to pattern his declaration of independence directly on the United States Declaration of Independence. He called for the same basic rights and freedoms in an effort to illustrate that his course was fundamentally the same as that of the original American colonies. In the general election which followed, Ho Chi Minh and the Viet Minh won an overwhelming victory, taking almost all the seats in their National Assembly. In his new capacity as president of the Democratic Republic of Viet Nam Ho

Left: Nguyen Xuan Thuy addresses a session of the World Council of Peace at Vienna on the Vietnamese problem in November 1953.

Above: French troops comb through a jungle thicket in search of Viet Minh snipers during Operation Lorraine in January 1953.

Chi Minh called for the immediate withdrawal of France from Indochina. However Ho Chi Minh made one serious miscalculation. He assumed that the United States would continue to support his justifiable cause of independence as it had supported him against Japan. What he failed to realize fully was that in the immediate postwar era anti-Fascism was replaced by anti-Communism. The United States would no longer support Ho Chi Minh's cause, however just it may have appeared. It was a bitter blow to Ho, The American OSS teams and advisors were withdrawn by the end of 1945 and the French found that with their departure the weight behind the Viet Minh was gone.

fact that, although many people supported the Viet Minh, the nationalistic movement was strong only in the industrial northern provinces of Vietnam around Hanoi. In the agricultural southern and coastal areas, particularly in the region between the ancient capital of Hue and the city of Saigon, the people appeared content to allow the French to resume control while they quietly hoped for independence without major confrontation.

On 2 September 1945 Ho Chi Minh proclaimed the Democratic Republic of Viet Nam and called for the abdication of the absent puppet emperor of the French and Japanese, Bao Dai. In doing so he declared the right of self-determination for the Vietnamese people, with or without French consent. Ho Chi Minh realized

In the months that followed, the French agreed to recognize the Republic, with the stipulation that it could not be divorced from France, and also agreed that a referendum would be held in the 'near future' to determine if the people of Vietnam wanted to remain under the protection of France or be independent under Ho Chi Minh's nationalist government. Negotiations in Hue and Paris broke down in 1946 as neither side was willing to compromise. In parts of Vietnam fighting broke out between Viet Minh and French troops. These confrontations were primarily confined to the northern provinces as Ho Chi Minh had relocated around Hanoi, leaving the French with a power base in the south and a colonial government in Saigon.

For the next seven years the French and their Vietnamese allies in the south were at war with the Viet Minh. Although the military situation weighed heavily in favor of the French, the Viet Minh showed no signs of acknowledging this or relinquishing their struggle. Although the French might have superior weapons and equipment, Ho Chi Minh held the superior long-term position. He understood the complexities of the situation, primarily the fact that without the support of the population it would be impossible for the French to hold all the key areas or deny the Viet Minh their traditional power base in the north. Thus Ho Chi Minh's strategy was to harass and frustrate the French at every turn, denying them a safe haven in Vietnam. If the Viet Minh and other guerrilla forces could accomplish this then Ho Chi Minh was certain that the frustration could lead them to one of two courses. Either the French would tire of the ceaseless struggle and leave Vietnam or they

would make a strategic error which the Viet Minh could turn to their advantage. The French, on the other hand, adopted a policy of holding the main cities and keeping primary routes of communication and transportation open while waiting for a large, set battle in which the superior French arms and army could destroy the nationalist movement. One issue was common to both strategies. Each side hoped that the other would make an error which would ultimately lead to its demise.

General Vo Nguyen Giap, commander of the Viet Minh military arm, continued the patient erosion of the French military and political position while he waited for an opportunity to give his army a clear victory. In 1953 the opportunity came. The French government had appointed General Henri Eugéne Navarre commander of all French forces in Indochina. Navarre understood the political mood that was evolving in France and realized that the precarious situation in Indochina must be brought to a swift, profitable conclusion. On his arrival he assessed the strengths and weaknesses of the French position. The Viet Minh had been permitted to wage their guerrilla war from the countryside and had been able to choose their terms and points of attack, always placing the French at a disadvantage, where the full weight of the French military strength could not be utilized. Finally,

secure the area. Over the next two days more men and supplies arrived, bringing the total French forces to approximately 5000 men. From their base the French began to mount reconnaissance missions which were generally futile, but they remained supremely confident. In the meantime Giap concentrated on en-

the guerrillas had time, something which the French people seemed unwilling to give their government. Navarre believed his strength lay in the French military machine and 'superior' intellect. He was certain that if he could tempt the Viet Minh into a set battle they would be destroyed with very little effort. He carefully baited a trap which the Viet Minh could not resist. A large French airborne assault force was to be dropped into the deserted airfield of a valley in northwestern Vietnam, the guerrillas' base. They were to establish fortifications around the airfield, which would also be their supply link. The Viet Minh could not ignore such a situation in their own back yard and Navarre was confident that the Viet Minh would be easily defeated when they attempted to attack the airfield defenses. The impending battle, considered one of the great military actions of the twentieth century, became known as Dien Bien Phu.

Plans for Operation Castor were drafted and on 20 November 1953 three French and Vietnamese paratroop battalions totalling 1800 men were air dropped at Dien Bien Phu. The careful planning immediately went awry as a Viet Minh regiment in the valley opened fire on the paratroopers. The cargo and heavy weapons dropped with the soldiers were scattered around the valley. One paratroop battalion's drop was mismanaged and they too were scattered. In spite of the handicaps of the drop the French managed to

circling Dien Bien Phu with more heavy guns (carried to the valley by mule or human bearers) and men than the French ever suspected possible. As Giap strengthened his position it became evident that the French were having severe logistics problems. The French engineers had indicated that 36,000 tons of materiel were needed to adequately fortify and defend Dien Bien Phu. Their isolation meant that every ounce had to be flown in by fixed-wing cargo aircraft. When Giap was ready to attack only 4000 tons of the French materiel had arrived.

By March 1954 the French had established eight perimeter bases around the Dien Bien Phu airstrip and one base further south as a guard for their only avenue of retreat if anything went wrong. The bases were manned by 6500 French regulars, legionaires and allied forces. At 1715 hours on 13 March the Viet Minh began their siege of Dien Bien Phu. Within 48 hours two of the outposts had been overrun and the others were taking a pounding from the Viet Minh artillery. French reinforcements were flown in on 16 March but at the same time the Thai allies deserted *en masse*. Throughout the remainder of March the French defended their positions against overwhelming odds, forcing the Viet Minh to pay dearly for each attempt to assault the defenses. Giap decided to rest and reconsolidate his forces and April proved relatively quiet.

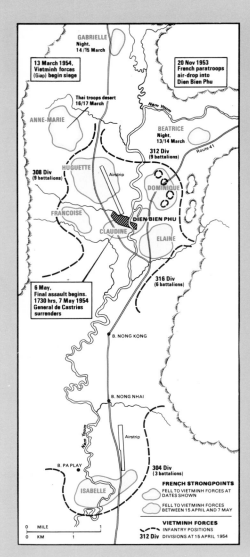

Above: a map of the Battle of Dien Bien Phu.

Above right: Viet Minh examine captured French rifles.

On 1 May the Viet Minh assaults began again in earnest and continued until 8 May when the last position, outpost Isabelle, fell. Although it took 56 days for the Viet Minh to crush the French defenses, from the outset there had been little doubt that they eventually would succeed. The French troops and some of their allies at the site fought with a staunch determination that earned them a place in history, but their commanders and government had failed them. The commanders of the Dien Bien Phu operation and subsequent relief and evacuation attempts, Operations Condor and Albatross, demonstrated a lack of appreciation of the determination and ingenuity of their adversary. Their ignorance of the massive logistic coordination necessary to assure victory was overwhelming. The French had come to believe their own propaganda about the inferiority of the Asian people, which contributed to their defeat.

The loss at Dien Bien Phu made the desired French position unattainable. The power had shifted to the Viet Minh and the Democratic Republic of Vietnam. On 20 June 1954 in Geneva, Switzerland, the concerned parties met to establish an agreement which would allow a smooth transition of power and the end of colonial rule. The Geneva Agreement of 1954 was a lengthy document but its primary points were clear. French Indochina was to be divided into four parts along national boundaries. Laos and Cambodia were to be separate entities and Vietnam itself was divided along the seventeenth parallel. The northern section was to be governed by the Viet Minh and the southern region was to remain temporarily under French control with Bao Dai as emperor once again. A demilitarized zone was created between the two. The Geneva Agreement also stated that in 1956 elections would be held to determine if the country would be reunited.

Ho Chi Minh wanted all the country under his government, not half. Within the two years he intended to consolidate and coordinate his power structure, secure in the belief that when the election was held the people would rally behind him. Although the agreement reached was the only one which the French would sign, it was only a temporary answer.

2 CONTAINING COMMUNISM

With the signing of the Geneva Agreement it appeared that the Vietnam issue had been resolved and that the country would finally be at peace. However although the agreement might have been a step in the right direction it also created several problems. Vietnam had been divided along economic boundaries. The northern region was traditionally the industrial center, with the natural resources available to support it. The south, primarily the Mekong Delta, was the agricultural base of the country. Neither country could survive on its own. For this reason if for no other the Communist faction, whose leadership had brought independence from French rule, felt certain of victory in the 1956 referendum and were not overly concerned with long-term consequences.

The division also created a major population shift within the country. The large Catholic population of the North, which had supported the French, feared retaliation by the Communists and 85 percent of the Catholics had migrated to the South by 1956. Some 100,000 Viet Minh guerrillas and supporters in the South, their dream of a nationalist state realized in the North, began their trek to the provinces around Hanoi to help build their new country. However, some 5000 Viet Minh regulars were ordered by Ho Chi Minh to remain in the South. They were to be a political force, known by their reputations as strong leaders, in the impending elections, but would become the cadre when the elections were cancelled.

However Ho Chi Minh failed to recognize that a technicality would be used against him on the referendum issue. As he was actively building his own country the French were leaving South Vietnam. By 1956 the French had departed and of the Geneva Agreement signatories only Ho Chi Minh remained. A new South Vietnamese government, supported by the Eisenhower Administration, was in power. Self-proclaimed premier Ngo Dinh Diem had attracted the attention and support of the United States as a strong, anti-Communist leader with the political and military power to control his new nation. As the date for the referendum approached, Diem cancelled the elections on the grounds that neither he nor his American allies had signed the agreement and therefore were not bound by it. The seeds of conflict were sown and a bitter hatred grew between Ho Chi Minh's government and South Vietnam and the United States.

Not only were problems beginning to develop in Vietnam. The other sectors created by the Geneva Agreement were being drawn into the Cold War. All over the world the United States and Soviet Union were allying themselves with other nations. The antagonism between the United States and Soviet Union launched both into a series of confrontations. Perhaps the most destructive path ever taken by American foreign policy makers was taken in this phase of the Cold War. Decisions to support nations around the world were not based on whether their governments had the support of the masses or were in the best interests of the people, nor even if they followed the basic principles that the American people held so

Below: Vietnam at the time of the French withdrawal, 1954.

11

dear. The sole criteria for United States support was whether the government professed pro- or anti-Communist sympathies. By using such limited principles the United States permitted corrupt governments to flourish under American support as long as they were willing to stand against the enemy, Communism. The dread of Communism during the Eisenhower era gave rise to a political idea which continues to have effect – the Domino Theory. This states that if the 'Free World' does not meet every challenge presented by the Communist faction, then Communism will take control of country after country in a 'fall of dominoes pattern' until the chain reaction is broken or all have fallen. Unfortunately the United States paid little attention to the needs of the various peoples so long as the Communists did not take control.

It was thus inevitable that the Vietnam conflict would involve the United States. However direct American involvement in Southeast Asia began with Laos, Vietnam's neighbor. Laos was then led by Prince Souvanna Phouma, who was making a desperate attempt to maintain a neutral position with a coalition government of pro-West and pro-Communist elements. The Communist faction, known as the Pathet Lao and supported by Communist China and North Vietnam, was headed by Souvanna Phouma's half-brother, Prince Souphanouvang. The pro-West faction was led by Prince Boun Oum, who also controlled the 25,000-man Royal Laotian Army, financed and equipped by the United States. From the Geneva Agreement until 1958 Laos was in constant turmoil as both factions struggled to gain control. In the 1958 elections Prince Souphanouvang won a resounding victory and American influence began to deteriorate proportionately. Prince Souvanna Phouma was persuaded to resign his position in favor of an American-backed successor, Phoui Sanaikone. He was able to sustain a neutral position by uniting several of the lesser political parties in Laos against Souphanouvang. However in 1959 the United States supported Phoui Sanaikone in a coup to depose the Communist leaders. Souphanouvang was arrested and the military arm of the Pathet Lao, which was being absorbed into the Royal Laotian Army, broke away and established a power base at the border of Laos and North Vietnam. In this remote area it felt relatively safe and was confident that it could launch guerrilla operations from its base, with arms and equipment supplied by the Communist Chinese and the Viet Minh if necessary. Over the next few months it became obvious that Souphanouvang's arrest meant a life sentence in prison and the Pathet Lao began operations. Almost one year after his arrest Souphanouvang escaped and joined the Pathet Lao in northern Laos.

Although it appeared that the pro-West faction had control, many called for the resumption of a neutral coalition. Led by a young captain of the elite Paratroop Battalion of the Royal Laotian Army a coup succeeded

Above: an ARVN soldier guards captured VC guerrillas.

Above right: a blindfolded VC suspect awaits interrogation.

in seizing the Laotian capital, Vientiane. The United States was embarrassed by the coup, which placed Prince Souvanna Phouma once more at the head of a coalition government that had the support not only of the Soviet Union but of American Western allies, primarily France and Britain. A unanimous call was made for the United States to stop its meddling in Laotian affairs. The United States and Thailand stood firm in their support of the anti-Communist faction in Laos. The Soviet Union responded by taking an active support role, flying supplies from North Vietnam to the rebel paratroopers in Vientiane. The United States reacted by supporting the Royal Laotian Army in an open confrontation with the paratroopers for control of the government and Vientiane. The weight of the Royal Laotian Army's attack was more than the rebels could withstand. They gave up the capital and retreated to form yet another power base in the north central region called the Plain of Jars. The pro-West elements again took control but the neutralists and the Pathet Lao had united against them. The United States then began to send not only weapons, equipment and aircraft, but also advisors to the Royal Laotian Army, increasing its involvement. The North Vietnamese cadre moved across the border into Laos to help train the Pathet Lao. Communist support had been subtle but the confrontations had forced all the concerned parties into blatant support.

However none of the three primary governments involved, the United States, the Soviet Union and the North Vietnamese, was willing to acknowledge the next phase of escalation. The situation had become so volatile that the only means of breaking the deadlock was to commit combat troops. The United States recognized that such a move would be fraught with difficulties. Laos was a land-locked country, and although American troops could be placed there supplies would cause problems. The Royal Laotian Army was a disappointment to the United States and it was feared that if American troops were committed they would be forced to carry the burden of the conflict. Also American strategic reserves were focussed on Europe, in case of an outbreak of hostilities with the Soviet Union. Finally, and perhaps most importantly, the United States could find no support among its Western allies. America had no desire to be branded the aggressor in Laos. In short the United States was forced to admit that Laos simply was not worth the risk. The Soviet Union found its position virtually identical to the United States' but with one major difference. The Soviet Union realized that once American support was withdrawn the neutralists and Communists would gain the upper hand and was satisfied with that prospect. Only the North Vietnamese were in a location actively to support the Pathet Lao, but they had neither the equipment nor the finances to do so.

The result was that in May 1961 conferences were held in Geneva which reaffirmed the independence of Laos. The Laotian Accords contained four basic points: a declaration of Laotian neutrality; an edict to respect that neutrality and refrain from interference in Laotian affairs; a halt to all military aid to Laos; and the establishment of a new government in Laos. The government, with Prince Souvanna Phouma at its head, Prince Souphanouvang as second in command and Phoumi Nosavan, strongly pro-West, as the head of financial affairs, was intended to maintain a neutral stance. However, Phoumi Nosavan struck out to achieve a quick victory over the neutralists and Communists, apparently confident that the United States would support him. He was wrong. In May 1962 his coup was crushed, bringing an end to the

civil war in Laos, but no end to the chaos that afflicted the country.

In the United States President John F Kennedy took the reins of American foreign policy with his election in 1960. He regarded the Laotian incidents as a major setback to his international position. The situation in Laos was given a back seat to the fiasco of the Bay of Pigs Invasion of Cuba, but they were both detrimental to Kennedy's position nonetheless. In an effort to regain a strong anti-Communist footing, the Kennedy Administration transferred its attention and support from Laos to Diem's government in South Vietnam. In Vietnam Kennedy foresaw allied support, particularly from the French, in the event of direct confrontation with Hanoi. Vietnam had the advantage which Laos lacked of an extremely long coastline with ports capable of supplying combat troops. Its political situation would also allow for various methods of American support.

By the time the shift from Laos to Vietnam occurred there were approximately 600 Communist incidents per month. It was estimated that 75 percent of the country was under guerrilla control. Although the United States ambassador to South Vietnam, Frederick E Nolting, indicated that there was widespread dissatisfaction with the Diem family regime, and the government of South Vietnam could be called undesirable at best, it fullfilled America's criteria of being willing to continue to fight against the Communist movement. In May 1961, before the Laotian issue was finally settled, Kennedy sent Vice-President Lyndon Johnson to Saigon to discover what Diem wanted and needed to combat the Communist threat to his country. Johnson was also to analyze the ability of the South Vietnamese army to fight the guerrillas. Perhaps most importantly, Johnson had to convince Diem that the United States' offer of full support was serious and it would not abandon Vietnam as it apparently had Laos.

Although Johnson offered Diem troops he refused, instead requesting more equipment and more money, to increase the Army of the Republic of Vietnam (ARVN) by 30,000 and to establish a 60,000-man civil guard to protect the rural villages from the guerrillas. Diem was also willing to accept American advisors who specialized in flight training, support activities, maintenance and command and administration. Limited numbers of advisors would not be able to undermine Diem's own army's capabilities, on which his power and support depended.

When Johnson returned to the United States he informed Kennedy of Diem's requests and said that something had to be done immediately to bolster the South Vietnamese government's position. Kennedy decided to send General Maxwell Taylor to assess the United States' alternatives in increasing the operational capacity of the ARVN. Taylor's arrival heralded the institution of a new American agency, the Military Assistance Command Vietnam (MACV), whose responsibility it would be to assist the South Vietnamese in their war effort. MACV was to replace the

old Military Assistance and Advisory Group (MAAG) which had been the ARVN's primary support since the French left Vietnam.

Increased military aid to the South by 1962 caught Ho Chi Minh off guard and the Diem regime began to counter successfully the guerrilla movement. However the basic problems of South Vietnam remained. The people of South Vietnam had no confidence in their corrupt government and, in spite of the fact that Diem thought military victory would bring him loyalty, sought the social reforms that had been promised. Although Diem assured the United States that reforms were forthcoming he continued to find excuses for failing to implement them. The situation produced anger among his people. One 'reform' which was implemented was the creation of the 'fortified hamlet.' Throughout the country people were relocated from their villages into government-controlled hamlets to 'protect' them from the guerrillas. The majority of people saw the scheme as a means of

Left: a guard patrols the fortified perimeter of an outpost.
Below left: South Vietnamese local militia receive instruction in marksmanship.

bidden the ARVN to risk life and equipment. American lives were lost and the media used the event to attack Diem again, accusing him of rewarding officers who did nothing and supressing and even reprimanding officers who showed leadership. It was obvious that the war could not be won in this manner, but Diem feared that a popular military leader might rise to favor and topple his regime.

Again Kennedy found himself with what appeared to be another foreign policy disaster. Fifty American lives had been lost so far and more than $4,000,000 had been pumped into Diem's government. Yet the guerrillas still controlled the countryside, the South Vietnamese Army refused to fight, and the people hated their government and now the United States more than ever. The media repeatedly stated that the United States should either take control of the war and win it or get out all together. This mood was reflected in the Kennedy Administration. The 1964 presidential campaign was just around the corner and if Kennedy was to be reelected he had to prove himself a true leader at home and abroad.

It was evident that Diem had no intention of changing his position or policies. Throughout the summer of 1963 South Vietnam was in turmoil as the Buddhist minority and the Catholic majority in cities clashed over religious freedoms and political control. Diem's regime increasingly repressed the Buddhists and the media and American newsmen had to smuggle stories and film out of the country. The Kennedy Administration tried to change course by replacing Nolting with Henry Cabot Lodge and by replacing General Harkins as Chief US Military Commander, but it had little positive effect. It was becoming obvious that Diem would have to be removed. On 1 November 1963 General Duong Van Minh staged a coup. After a brief confrontation around the presidential palace the generals took control, though Diem and his brother fled to the Chinese quarter of Saigon. When they realized that there could be no escape the two men surrendered, assuming that they would be given safe conduct into exile. Once in the hands of the new government both men were executed.

Exactly three weeks after the coup in Saigon, which allegedly he had supported and authorized, President John F Kennedy died of an assassin's bullet. As the new government formed in South Vietnam, headed by General Duong Van Minh, 'Big Minh,' a new Administration took over in Washington. The change in Saigon was expected to solve the problems. The change in Washington placed Lyndon B Johnson, a man with the same political aspirations as his predecessor, in command of the increasingly difficult situation in Southeast Asia.

maintaining strict control over the peasant population of South Vietnam. The people blamed not only Diem but the United States, who they began to look upon as another enemy, relocating them against their wishes. The 'fortified hamlet' was a breeding ground for discontent which drove many to join the guerrillas.

The hostility to the Diem regime caught the attention of the American media. Accustomed to the freedom of the press enjoyed in the United States, the media found Diem's censorship intolerable and launched a campaign against him. Corruption and greed were exposed and the media went to great lengths to discover further evidence of the Diem family's misdeeds. The first major confrontation of ARVN troops with American advisors then occurred. In January 1963 plans were made for a combined ARVN and advisor offensive against a Communist position at Ap Boc. In the resulting battle the ARVN and advisors were badly mauled by the Communist forces, primarily because Diem had expressly for-

3 THE UNDECLARED WAR

The Diem regime had been eliminated but in January 1964 student riots and civil unrest extended from Saigon to Hue, throwing the country into turmoil once again. The United States had believed that the generals, led by 'Big Minh,' could initiate the necessary changes in South Vietnam but it was soon apparent that the new leaders had little desire for change. The coup failed to produce a renaissance, amounting to the substitution of one greedy head of state for another. The guerrillas took advantage of the South Vietnamese government's instability and launched a full-scale campaign to gain quick victories which would give them leverage in the future. Rumors began to spread through South Vietnam that 'Big Minh' and his colleagues were actually formulating plans for a coalition with the Communists and were almost ready for the transition. This was of course totally unacceptable to Washington. The obvious answer was

to support yet another coup in the hope that a new leadership would halt the disasterous landslide of events.

On 30 January 1964 Major General Nguyen Khanh executed a successful bloodless coup, deposing the 'Big Minh' government. Although General Khanh was not the favorite choice of President Johnson there was no other immediate alternative. The United States feared that if it did not support Khanh's new government, South Vietnam would dissolve into factions over which the United States could extend no control. If such a division occurred it was believed that it would take only a few months for many of the factions to unite with the Communists. Johnson wanted surface stability at any price and if Khanh could bring order to the chaos then the Johnson Administration would support him. In opposition circles it was rapidly becoming evident that the issue

Johnson ordered increased aid to South Vietnam. However, throughout February and into March the situation continued to deteriorate. In March Johnson sent Secretary of State Robert McNamara to South Vietnam on a fact-finding mission to determine what could be done to restore equilibrium to the country. McNamara's reports indicated that aid to South Vietnam had to be increased by approximately $60,000,000,000 and that equipment, including aircraft, infantry weapons and armored fighting vehicles, had to be upgraded if the South Vietnamese were to gain an advantage over the enemy. It was also estimated that the ARVN would need 50,000 more men in its ranks and that the United States would have to take financial responsibility for those troops.

Although it appeared that Johnson was merely increasing the amount of American aid, he had another plan in mind – retaliatory air strikes against North Vietnam. Johnson and his advisors agreed that some sort of pressure had to be brought against the Communists in the North to relieve the pressure on the South. Air strikes seemed to be the fastest, most effective means of accomplishing that goal. Air strikes would demonstrate to North Vietnam that the United States was embarking on a 'get tough' policy and would also provide a positive display of support for Khanh's government. The problem was that air strikes had not yet been considered or supported by Congress or the American people. If the approach to air attacks was not properly managed Johnson would find himself labelled a warmonger – and that would cost him the election. However, if he could justify the air war as a reprisal to acts of aggression committed by the Communists, then Johnson would be heralded as a defender of freedom and democracy.

By July 1964 the South had reached a critical point. Khanh, who had been given privileged information on the bombing strategy, publicly pressured the United States to act. He persistently repeated that the growing conflict in Vietnam was not merely the South Vietnamese government against the guerrillas and Hanoi but a confrontation between pro- and anti-Communist factions on a global scale. Other members of Khanh's government took up the cry and the media was swamped by the South Vietnamese officials' demands that the United States take direct action against the North. Johnson had to act. He first replaced Ambassador Lodge with General Maxwell Taylor, assigning General William Westmoreland as the new commander of the MACV program. With the change, a plan of high priority and sensitivity was put into motion. Under the title OPLAN 34, clandestine raids into North Vietnam were to be made. American and South Vietnamese operations were combined for surreptitious commando activities. The idea was to fight fire with fire – South Vietnamese commandos would retaliate with guerrilla attacks in the North. The United States was to fly reconnaissance missions over

Left: Vietnamese troops of the 21st Division surround a village suspected of giving shelter to the VC.

Above: ARVN troops depended on the United States for arms and equipment and often were led by US Army advisors.

was not simply the freedom of the South Vietnamese to maintain a position of self-determination as opposed to Communist rule. Two American Presidents staked their political reputations on the outcome and ego was governing where common sense and logic should have.

Johnson realized that the world was watching Vietnam. The reputation of the United States as an anti-Communist world power was at stake and he refused to let it be said that while he was president he let Vietnam fall. To maintain an aura of stability and to ensure his own reelection in November 1964, the North to report enemy infiltration points and areas of enemy troop buildup. In addition American and Thai pilots were to fly bombing missions from Laotian airfields to strike targets in the North. The 25–40 bombers were to bear Laotian markings to make it seem that the Royal Laotian Army had also actively joined the fight against the Communists. The final phase of OPLAN 34 called for American naval vessels, primarily destroyer-class ships, to patrol the coast of North Vietnam and gather intelligence, harass North Vietnamese shipping and support the commando raids whenever possible. It was this part of OPLAN 34 which would give Johnson the excuse he needed to launch America into the war.

On 2 August the destroyer USS *Maddox* was attacked by North Vietnamese patrol boats while on patrol in the Gulf of Tonkin. Two days later six patrol boats assaulted the *Maddox* and the USS *Turner Joy*. Although neither vessel suffered major damage, the engagement lasted for several hours and four of the North Vietnamese patrol boats were destroyed. On 5 August American aircraft retaliated by striking against North Vietnamese naval installations, destroying 25 vessels, most of which had little military significance. A major oil-storage depot was also attacked and two American aircraft were lost. With the loss of these crews the story was released to the press. The Gulf of Tonkin incident was reported as an unprovoked attack on American vessels for which the navy retaliated. Johnson immediately set about making the most of the situation, producing the Southeast Asian Resolution, better known as the Gulf of Tonkin Resolution. This document was to become the keystone of American involvement in Southeast Asia. Carefully worded so that it was not an actual declaration of war, the resolution made it possible for the United States to aid an ally which was defending itself from external forces. The speed with which the Southeast Asian Resolution reached Congress would seem to indicate that it had been drafted and was merely waiting for the right incident to be produced. Although originally denied, later information revealed that the American destroyers were in fact operating within the 15-mile limit of North Vietnamese territorial waters and that the North had been goaded into playing directly into Johnson's hands. Congress ratified the resolution and Johnson no longer had to be so cautious about the aid and support troops he sent to South Vietnam.

Johnson now had Congress and the American people behind him, but with only two and a half months until the elections he stated that while he had no intention of taking America into war he would not allow the United States to be pushed around. Senator Barry Goldwater, the Republican candidate for president, was defeated largely because he openly voiced his support for direct and massive military action in Vietnam. After his victory in the elections Johnson could follow the course he had always

intended. Opinion polls indicated that although the American people did not want a war they were confident that the United States could easily defeat the Communist aggressors in Vietnam and were in favor of positive action to reassert American superiority in the international community.

Although the Gulf of Tonkin Resolution gave Johnson the power openly to commit American troops to Southeast Asia, he was still faced with the problem of increasing American forces and involvement without appearing as the antagonist in an already volatile situation. The immediate method of involving American military might was to implement the air strike plan. However the Khanh government favored a march north now that the Johnson Administration had the power to commit combat troops. Khanh's plan was to sweep north to overwhelm the Communists and take the war to their own land. This strategy called for massive numbers of American troops to ensure its success, which was not Johnson's idea of the proper course for the moment. Johnson had to maintain his position as the benevolent protector or the situation could deteriorate as it had done in Laos. If the American president was portrayed as the aggressor popular opinion would swing against him, which would have meant political suicide for Johnson's Administration. Thus in late December 1964 Johnson decided to follow Maxwell Taylor's suggestion of bombing pretargeted strategic areas. Dubbed Operation Barrelroll the bombings were to be directed at the Ho Chi Minh Trail, the major supply route which ran parallel to South Vietnam through Laos from North Vietnam, with branches which crossed the border to support the guerrilla operations in the South. Johnson kept a tight though subtle rein on media coverage of

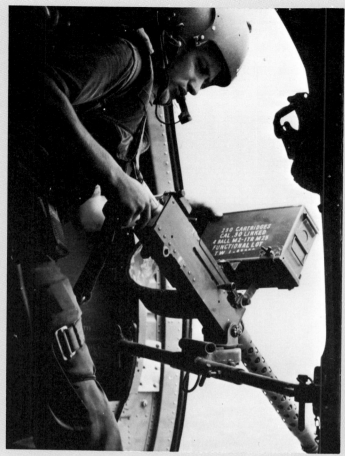

Left: a Montagnard fortified village viewed from the gunner's position of a US Army H-21 helicopter in February 1963.

Right: a helicopter gunner returns enemy fire.
Below: CH-21 troop-carrying helicopters gave ARVN forces a measure of air mobility.

the bombings, ensuring that they showed support for South Vietnam while displaying great restraint on the part of his Administration.

Although the Gulf of Tonkin Resolution and the bombings indicated American support for Khanh's government there were again political undercurrents in Saigon. Young officers, known as the Young Turks, were disillusioned by Khanh's methods and approach to the war. Nguyen Cao Ky, a young air force general, approached Westmoreland with the idea of a bloodless coup. However neither Westmoreland nor Taylor thought that South Vietnam would be better off with the Young Turks than with Khanh. Stability remained the crucial aim in the South and a compromise was made with the Young Turks. American aid would be increased in return for the generals' working toward a peaceful settlement of their differences with the welfare of their country in mind. Although on the surface there seemed to be solidarity in the government, the Young Turks were pressuring Khanh to replace what they considered to be the undesirable elements of his senior staff and generals. Khanh made gestures which appeased the Young Turks but he was merely biding his time. When it became apparent that he had no intention of cooperating with the young officers they again approached Ambassador Taylor to discuss a coup. Taylor is said to have informed General Ky that the Young Turks were naive schoolboys who did nothing more than threaten the stability of their country. He in turn threatened to put an immediate halt to American aid if the feuding within the South Vietnamese command and government did not cease. The Young Turks were furious but their hands were tied. Taylor realized the explosive possibilities of the situation and suggested to Khanh that he should perhaps step aside and allow a new coalition to form. Khanh, falsely secure in his position, decided to put Taylor in his place by releasing the details of their confidential meeting to the press. Khanh's ploy backfired and the United States stood firmly behind Taylor, letting it be known that if the petty squabbling did not cease immediately and if a stable government was not formed, then all military and financial aid to the country would end. It was obvious that American support for Khanh's regime was rapidly waning.

To further add to the confusion, Vietcong guerrillas bombed an hotel in Saigon on Christmas Eve 1964. Three Americans were killed and 51 American and South Vietnamese officers were injured. The bombing of the hotel, which was principally inhabited by American officers, was a direct attack on the United States and as it occurred in the South Vietnamese capital it was used to illustrate the ineffectiveness of Khanh's dealing with the terrorists. Although the

American secretary of state and the ambassador and military advisors in Vietnam urged Johnson to begin the air strikes on the North in retaliation for the bombing, Johnson continued to delay. He did not want to appear to be looking for any excuse to carry the war to North Vietnam, nor did he want it to be implied that Khanh himself might have had a hand in the bombing to prompt the instigation of the air war in a bid to bolster his failing position.

When the airstrikes did not materialize, and it was, as Johnson had feared, suggested that the hotel incident had been carried out by feuding factions of Khanh's government, Khanh was forced to resign in favor of a civilian government. Premier Tran Van Huong took control and although the government was clearly stable, another problem arose. The Buddhists rose up as they had done under the Diem regime, and refused to acknowledge or cooperate with Huong's government. They demanded the return of Khanh and early 1965 saw massive demonstrations and civil unrest throughout South Vietnam. The guerrillas took advantage of the chaos and attacked a small village near Saigon. Their operation was extremely successful and they occupied Binh Gia, killing some 200 ARVN troops and six Americans. Despite efforts to overcome the guerrillas, the battle ended only when the Vietcong, who were armed with the latest equipment supplied by the North, voluntarily withdrew from the area.

The battle at Binh Gia sent shockwaves through South Vietnam and the United States. It was clear that South Vietnam could not protect itself and that the Vietcong were becoming bolder every day. With the continued chaos in the South Vietnamese government, growing anti-American sentiments, the escalation of the war by the guerrillas and the direct attacks on American military personnel, Johnson decided that the time to act was drawing near. He had the support of the majority of Congress and the American people, but he wanted to be certain of that support and so allowed the anger of the American populace to build. With the commencement of the Tet Lunar New Year Holiday truce in January 1965 the Vietcong attacked the American advisors' compound at Pleiku, killing two and wounding more than 100 American soldiers. The guerrillas also mounted a major offensive in Binh Dinh Province where ARVN forces suffered more than 500 casualties. These attacks occurred while the Soviet Premier Alexei Kosygin was visiting Hanoi. Johnson had his long-awaited incident. He could now say that the attacks were definitely Soviet inspired and that America had no choice but to retaliate against North Vietnam and send even more aid to the South to oppose Communist threat.

America embarked on an air war that had two primary goals, to punish North Vietnam for each act of aggression committed by Communist forces in the South and, more importantly, to attack the 94 military

and industrial centers which had directly supported the guerrillas. Johnson was confident that the air war alone would be sufficient to smash the North Vietnamese economic and military positions, which would lead to the collapse of the guerrilla movement in South Vietnam. However another aspect of the air war caused a major shift in American policy. American air bases were established and strengthened to enable aircraft to fly directly from South Vietnam and General Westmoreland called for American combat troops to protect them. He realized that once American aircraft began bombing the North the air bases would become primary targets for the guerrillas. The ARVN simply could not offer adequate protection.

Thus on 26 February 1965 Johnson approved a bill to provide American ground troops for the defense of American airfields. On 8 March US marines landed at China Beach, just outside Da Nang. The Da Nang air base was one of the largest in the northern provinces of South Vietnam and would therefore attract a great deal of attention from the guerrillas. The 9th Marine Expeditionary Brigade made a full

combat assault of China Beach – to the cheers of American Air Force personnel and the bewildered stares of South Vietnamese civilians. The assault on a completely secure beach, decorated with signs saying 'Welcome Gallant Marines' was a mock display of strength which ended in a party atmosphere. The arrival of combat forces, whose stated role was strictly defensive, opened the door for direct ground intervention in Vietnam. The North Vietnamese responded to the marines' arrival by sending the first North Vietnamese army regulars, known to the Americans as the NVA, officially and blatantly into the South. Within a year there was an estimated strength of three NVA infantry divisions in the South, as well as some 67,000 hardcore Vietcong and over 200,000 active sympathizers.

American troop commitment was carefully controlled. The troops' role was defensive, to keep the country secure until the ARVN could take control of the situation. However Johnson's military advisors had told him, as they had told Kennedy, that the ARVN was not capable of managing the war effort on its own. It had been repeatedly demonstrated that

ARVN troops were poorly trained, poorly led and in too many cases acted as if they cared little about the situation in their country. Too many were soldiers simply because it meant food, clothing and a place to sleep. However American advisors in Vietnam believed that given proper training, modern equipment and good leadership, the ARVN could someday shoulder the war's responsibilities. Until then that weight would have to be carried by the American infantryman. Johnson knew that the success of the Vietnam venture rested on increased American combat support and to legitimize this he called on America's SEATO allies to join the battle against Communism. With allies in combat the United States could avoid being portrayed as the sole

by their government, even though it was not their own government's troops who were providing that security. Search-and-destroy missions were also meant to show the guerrilla that the countryside was no longer a safe haven and that he was now facing an enemy that would deliberately engage him on his own ground. After the initial surprise effects of the search-and-destroy missions it was soon evident that the theory had several major flaws. Quite simply, the guerrilla was not bound to engage the mission forces. All that the Communist forces had to do was fade deeper into the countryside or enter the local civilian population until the American troops had passed, then reconsolidate to continue operations as before.

The American command believed that if the rural

Above left: a boarding party questions the crew of a junk off South Vietnam.

Above: monitors of the US Navy operated in the waterways of the Mekong Delta.

aggressive non-Communist force in Vietnam. Within months of the marine landing Australia and New Zealand had committed troops, and Nationalist China and South Korea had promised troops. In a sense Johnson had succeeded in giving Vietnam the appearance of another Korean 'police action,' with a group of nations taking a united stand against Communism.

The role of American ground troops changed rapidly. Their defensive postures were extended to cover the 'search-and-destroy' missions which would become so prevalent. Justified by the maxim, the 'best defense is a good offense,' American troops attacked the guerrillas. Initially the principal role of the search-and-destroy missions was to sweep an area around the base to locate and destroy all enemy forces or positions that the American troops encountered. The sector was then considered 'pacified.' The local population could then feel secure and supported

population could be led to believe that security truly existed under the new system then they would stop supporting the guerrilla and step forward to identify enemy troops. But for the most part the military misjudged the sentiments of the peasants, who had no love for either side and wanted only to be left in peace. They feared the guerrillas and they feared their own government and its allies. Perhaps most importantly, the memory of Diem's fortified hamlets reminded the peasants that the Vietcong at least did not force them from their villages. In the early days of involvement the Americans were learning the best tactics to use. However the needs of the people were largely ignored and America had no direction of purpose.

From July through September 1965 the influx of American combat troops continued with the 1st Infantry Division, the 101st Airborne Division, and the 1st Cavalry Division (Air Mobile) arriving. America was no longer limited to simply supporting and advising the South Vietnamese government and military. The United States had assumed a prominent combat role and although never declared, America was at war.

4 SEARCH AND DESTROY

In the autumn of 1965 the United States military became immersed in the Vietnam commitment. New strategies were being developed and implemented and Vietnam was seen as a quick and easy means to bolster American prestige around the world. The United States, as the leader of the anti-Communist sentiments of the Western World, was giving the Soviet Union a clear signal that America was serious in its bid to stop the Communists from gaining any advantage. Politically Johnson and his Administration saw the war not only in the light of its foreign position but also as it applied to important domestic issues. Victory in Vietnam would shift the country's attention from the pressing racial and civil rights issues. Quick victory would cover the Johnson Administration with enough glory to offset the negative social aspects being emphasized in the States.

In accepting the responsibility for the war the United States had placed itself in a very precarious position. The war in Vietnam had to be won. The ability of the United States to support its rhetoric with action in the Vietnam effort would be closely watched. If America was the cornerstone of democracy it claimed to be, then its fighting men were its strength. If the American soldier failed in Vietnam it would raise grave doubts about the nation's ability to maintain its NATO commitment, or any other commitments around the world. It could prove America's claim to be the world's leading superpower to be hollow. If America could not support its claims then there was only one other giant which could – the Soviet Union.

American military capability was being put to the test. The American strategy of being purely advisory had failed owing to corruption and lack of leadership. MacNamara's strategy had been for American troops to take the bulk of responsibility for the war to give the ARVN time to build its strength. The primary question was now whether or not the American military effort fitted the needs of the war being waged. The Communist movement was gaining ground around the world through guerrilla warfare and terrorism. If the United States, and subsequently the ARVN, failed in Vietnam it would force the United States to rethink its 'world protector' ideology and reveal America's inability to oppose Communist

Above: men of the Long Range Reconnaissance Patrol are signalled to halt and take cover by their leader, during a mission by the 1st Infantry Division in September 1967.

Above right: a trooper of the 173rd Airborne Brigade looks at a Vietcong artist's view of the American soldier, which was found in a deserted village.

Above far right: troops of the 11th Armored Cavalry Regiment take cover as VC automatic weapons open fire on them.

ventures around the world. The United States largely ignored the clear demonstration of the fact that the tactics used in Vietnam guerrilla fighting heralded a new era of warfare.

In spite of the long-term significance of Vietnam, the United States appeared to rush forward blindly. Although the search-and-destroy, and later reconnaissance in force, tactic was applied to counter the guerrilla, the United States soon slipped back into the strategy that had proved so disastrous for the French more than a decade before. Like the French, the dependent, relying on one another and main headquarters for artillery protection and supplies. Smaller, less permanent bases were simply extensions of larger bases. It was on the fire support bases that the men lived, fought and died, but their contribution was overshadowed by the major confrontations and activities around the large cities.

Finally, like the French, the Americans gave the guerrillas the initiative by relying on technological superiority to defeat their enemy. The United States placed great faith in technological advancement and

United States centered its power in the large cities and villages, sending enormous quantities of men and materiel to these areas while doing little to ensure the security of the outlying countryside. The guerrillas were not particularly interested in launching their terrorist attacks on the cities, nor did they consider urban areas to be essential targets, it was simply that the Americans had placed their troops there. Just as search-and-destroy and reconnaissance in force took the view that to eliminate the enemy one must go where he is, the guerrillas attacked the Americans where they were – in the urban areas.

When the American military ventured into the countryside it built fortified operation centers, called fire support bases, from whence to conduct missions against areas believed to be enemy lines of resupply or infiltration. Fire support bases, or fire bases, became to Vietnam what the trenches were to World War I. They covered the rural sectors and surrounded main divisional operation centers. The size, strength and permanence of fire support bases depended on their function. Troop numbers varied from several platoons to battalion strength. A battery of artillery, ranging from 105mm howitzers and mortars to 8-inch self-propelled guns occupied an entrenched or revetted position on the base. Each base had a tactical operations center to command and an intelligence headquarters. Larger fire support bases were inter-

in the ability of American industry to continue to produce new weapons. The American military prided itself on having the best-trained and equipped soldiers in the world, and some of the most sophisticated support equipment ever provided to troops in the field. All branches of the American military seemed to view Vietnam as a testing ground for new weapons, partly because it was the United States military not the United States which was at war. It was perhaps in this military aspect more than any other that America truly lost sight of its stated objectives in Vietnam.

From late 1965 through 1967 the United States was locked in a war of attrition with the Communist forces and most casualties were lost in action supporting the fire support bases. However in November 1965 the first set battle between American and North Vietnamese troops occurred in the Ia Drang Valley, some five miles from the Cambodian border. Vietcong and North Vietnamese volunteers clashed with the 1st Cavalry Division and, although American casualties are believed to have been heavy, no figure has ever been released. It is estimated that the NVA/VC lost some 1400 troops during the engagement. Both sides claimed victory in this battle, a circumstance which would prevail throughout the war.

Over the next two years the United States enemy remained elusive, attacking only when the odds were

distinctly in its favor or when a decisive political advantage could be gained. The fire support bases and the search-and-destroy missions were creating several problems. Intelligence reports about guerrilla positions and operations in sectors for which American forces were responsible were limited and often inaccurate, which meant that a large percentage of anti-guerrilla missions found nothing, which increased the frustration of the ground troops. More American casualties were sustained from terror tactics like sniper attacks and booby traps than in set battles. When search-and-destroy missions did contact the enemy it was usually in ambush, with the Americans in an extremely poor position and outside the immediate support range of other units. After brief encounters which sometimes lasted only several minutes the guerrillas would fade back into the countryside. It was not uncommon for small patrols to be wiped out to a man. The major complaint of American troops was that they knew they could defeat the enemy but just did not know how to make him stand and fight.

Therefore it was not the basic infantry tactics employed by the United States but the strength of support equipment and technology which inflicted the most damage on the Communist forces. Heavy bombers and long-range artillery were the primary

effective sources of offensive action against the guerrilla.

By the end of 1967 the war was a virtual stalemate. The Americans had crippled the Communist effort in spite of increased numbers of NVA troops participating in the war. The ARVN were taking a more prominent part though they were still not as reliable as other allied forces. The United States command was growing tired of the seemingly endless string of minor skirmishes which cost lives but accomplished little and searched for the set battle where superior American firepower and support technology could be used to advantage. Although the French had tried and failed to do this in the early 1950s, the helicopter and advances in field support made it a viable plan. Although it was unlikely that the American command would deliberately re-create a Dien Bien Phu situation, if one developed the United States had the technology to make a victory possible.

Perhaps the most noted change by late 1967 was Secretary of Defense McNamara's attempts to run the war like a large corporation, and technology was playing an ever larger part. Seismic and electronic sensors, as well as radar surveillence equipment was placed at strategic locations throughout South Vietnam to detect enemy movement and indicate troop concentrations. In some areas such detection methods replaced ground patrols. Whenever these systems registered movement the area would be saturated with aircraft and artillery fire. This did not always result in enemy losses as the delicate equipment often registered wild animals or even insects. Chemical warfare in the form of defoliants, such as Agent Orange, and cloud seeding to produce unnatural rainfall were also employed. Defoliants particularly were relatively untried and their long-term effects are only now being realized. The use of sophisticated weapons, such as bombs which could be guided to their targets via television screens in the aircraft, is an example of how the war was used as a proving ground.

McNamara was eager to illustrate the effectiveness of his 'corporate' strategy and did so by promoting the 'body count' program. Enemy kill figures were displayed as dividends of the new technological approach to war. The 'corporate' attitude even seeped through to the commitment and replacement of troops to South Vietnam. Men were sent to fill the slots in an assembly-line fashion. This replacement system destroyed the *esprit de corps* which affects the

manner in which units perform. Thus, while McNamara's figures continued to portray the war effort in a positive light, and he continued to assure the American people that the ARVN would soon be comprised of soldiers capable of fighting their own war, the situation really changed very little. The NVA/VC still held the countryside and sophisticated equipment and increased bombing raids failed to change this. Worse still, the media and Johnson's political opponents began to claim that McNamara's intelligence reports were being falsified to indicate a more favorable situation than existed. Reports claimed that McNamara's body count of enemy killed exceeded the entire population of North Vietnam. More questions were raised when CIA reports leaked to the media conflicted with official reports from the defense department. McNamara's activities fuelled the 'Big Lie' attitude taken by opponents to the war. This attitude hampered the United States' pursuit of victory in Vietnam.

In spite of the American military effort General Giap, who had led the Viet Minh so successfully against the French, saw that the war had begun to resemble the situation of the 1950s. The growing disenchantment and dissent in the United States, and the high level of frustration of American combat troops, led him to believe that the time was right to attempt another Dien Bien Phu. If he could launch

a major offensive which would produce a similar disaster, the United States might be forced to abandon South Vietnam as a hopeless cause. Added to this was the fact that the Johnson Administration was facing an election in 1968. If Giap could manipulate the Americans into a major military defeat, or even an operation which would humiliate Johnson and feed the growing peace movement in the United States, then the Communists' position in Vietnam would be virtually assured.

In October 1967 Giap issued a statement which predicted an imminent victory for the Communist cause. Although the American command had become accustomed to such rhetoric, a major enemy buildup was indicated in the northernmost province of Quang Tri. Giap appeared to be putting great effort into an offensive in the area surrounding the fire support base at Khe Sanh near the Laotian border. Giap's offensive would consist of two primary phases. The anticipated assault against Khe Sanh would begin in late 1967 and continue through April 1968. The more widely publicized phase, the Tet Offensive of 1968, would catch even the military experts by surprise.

Khe Sanh had originally been a special forces base, established to watch the Ho Chi Minh Trail which ran just across the border in Laos. It had also been a training center for the Montagnards, who inhabited the border areas of South Vietnam and Laos and had been recruited by special forces personnel as a counterguerrilla force. When the marines took posession of the base at Khe Sanh the special forces units moved even closer to the Laotian border, near the village of Lang Vei and began conducting their operations from that location. The marines converted Khe Sanh into a primary fire support base which could not only monitor enemy infiltration but also could launch attacks against the infiltration routes in the area. Khe Sanh was intended to be an irritant as well as a major offensive site. Air strikes launched from the airfield at Khe Sanh were intended to devastate the Ho Chi Minh Trail and seriously impede the flow of supplies to the guerrilla and NVA forces in the South.

By December 1967, although in complete command of their area, the marines and special forces began to notice a marked increase in enemy activity. Intelligence reported two elite NVA divisions in the immediate vicinity, the 325th and 304th NVA Regular Army Divisions, which 13 years earlier had fought at Dien Bien Phu. American forces in various sectors of eastern Quang Tri Province noticed heavy North Vietnamese infiltration across the DMZ, particularly near the 'Rock Pile,' a key point overlooking the primary land route, Route 9. It was obvious that a major offensive against Khe Sanh was imminent and that the forces entering across the DMZ intended to isolate the base from possible American reinforcements at Quang Tri and Dong Ha.

Khe Sanh was strikingly similar to Dien Bien Phu. It was a fortified area which surrounded an airfield and lay in a valley. It appeared that the Communists had an even greater advantage than they had had against the French at Dien Bien Phu, as Giap could position long-range artillery in the relatively safe DMZ, which had long been off limits to American bombers. Khe Sanh's position only a few miles from the Ho Chi Minh Trail would make resupply and reinforcement of the Communist forces relatively simple. However, as Giap closed the noose around Khe Sanh, he overlooked one crucial point. Although he positioned antiaircraft weapons in the hills around Khe Sanh to stop the Americans receiving air supplies, he misjudged American expertise in the utilization of the helicopter. This miscalculation, and the unexpected determination of American ground forces in the province, would cost the NVA/VC their victory at Khe Sanh.

The siege of Khe Sanh began on 21 January 1968, only three days after the halt to the bombing of Hanoi in preparation for the Tet Lunar New Year Holiday truce. The NVA/VC attacked the base at dawn and although they inflicted few casualties they destroyed the main storage depot and several helicopters. After the main assault was repulsed the NVA/VC launched probing attacks against the defenses of both Khe Sanh and Lang Vei. On 22 January the marine com-

Far left: 'tunnel rats' find
VC training aids during a
search mission.
Left: troops check a village
well which may conceal the
entrance to a VC tunnel.

Above: Private George Nagel
of the 173rd Airborne Brigade
puts to good use a sewing
machine found during the
search of a VC tunnel.

mander, acknowledging that a massive Communist offensive was underway, ordered his garrison forces to gather the local villagers into Khe Sanh for evacuation to Da Nang and Quang Tri. He stressed the importance of keeping the road between Khe Sanh and Lang Vei open. The garrison of the special forces base had increased sharply in the previous weeks as Royal Laotian Army troops sought refuge at Lang Vei after the Communists overran their border outpost, perhaps in an initial phase of the operations against the American positions. On 22 January 1500 reinforcements arrived at Khe Sanh, and the supplies were replaced by air.

On 23 January Intelligence reports estimated that some 18,000 NVA regulars surrounded Khe Sanh and were obviously waiting for the weather to change, which would nullify the American air superiority, to begin their attacks. Over the next two days the weather continued to deteriorate until the western half of Quang Tri Province and much of Laos was covered by a blanket of fog. The fog did not only provide cover for the Communist forces around Khe Sanh but also for the infiltration of additional troops and supplies from the Ho Chi Minh Trail. Khe Sanh was under constant bombardment and the NVA/VC forces moved to within 1000 meters of the airstrip.

On 26 January every available American aircraft flew missions over Khe Sanh. More than 450 missions were flown on that day alone, though many were forced to turn back by NVA/VC antiaircraft fire. As the air attacks continued South Vietnamese Rangers, said to be the elite troops of South Vietnam, were flown into Khe Sanh. The orders given to these troops give a clear indication of the anticipated situation at Khe Sanh. They were told to fill any gaps in the defenses made by the enemy and, more importantly, to fight to the last man if necessary.

After the initial attack, American troops from eastern Quang Tri Province were engaged in a major battle to reopen Route 9 so that supplies and reinforcements could get through if prolonged bad weather isolated Khe Sanh from air support. It was not until 26 January that any headway was made.

At the end of January intelligence sources, including the CIA, in Quang Tri Province were convinced that over 50,000 NVA/VC troops were in the province or poised to strike across the DMZ. It appeared that the North was prepared to wrest Quang Tri away from South Vietnam if it could. Khe Sanh became the center of attention. Giap had chosen the location for his second Dien Bien Phu, now all he had to do was achieve that success once more.

5 THE TET OFFENSIVE

Military commanders and the media were quick to realize the similarities between Khe Sanh and Dien Bien Phu and reflected on the damage that a defeat would do to the American position. The Communists would profit from the embarrassment of the United States, even if victory eluded them.

General Westmoreland was convinced that Khe Sanh was not the only element of Giap's plan. Intelligence reports indicated a heavy influx of men and materiel throughout South Vietnam. Westmoreland was convinced that Giap intended to put pressure on other strategic points to immobilize the Americans and prohibit the massive support operations to Khe Sanh. The Tet Lunar Truce did not include I Corps, whose command encompassed the five northernmost provinces of South Vietnam. Westmoreland ordered the troops in that sector to prepare for a Communist offensive. However others argued that the massive numbers of NVA/VC troops in the northern provinces demonstrated that the Communists were throwing everything they had into this offensive. There was no question about the weight of the offensive and, as it was believed that the NVA/VC had no great reserve, activity elsewhere in South Vietnam was thought to be the movement of secondary units filtering into the country. Unfortunately the United States military had begun to believe the doctored figures that had resulted from McNamara's demands. Now, when accurate Intelligence reports were desperately needed, no one seemed able to discover what the truth actually was.

The truth became evident on the morning of 30 January 1968 with the start of the Communist Tet Offensive. The attack came as a complete surprise to the Americans and South Vietnamese, who had been watching the northern provinces and anticipating nothing more than harassment elsewhere in the South. NVA/VC forces attacked all the major cities and villages in force, from the northernmost city of Dong Ha to the Mekong Delta and Cau Mau. In spite of the diversity of attacks two areas were soon seen as the primary targets, Saigon and the ancient capital city, Hue. Although it would later become evident that the attacks in the other cities were too small to accomplish much against their intended targets, all were well coordinated and not merely ad hoc attacks

Above: a platoon from the 3rd Battalion, 7th Infantry Regiment, patrols through the deserted streets of the Saigon suburb of Cholon during the 1968 Tet offensive.

Above right: South Vietnam at the time of the Tet offensive. Right: soldiers of the US 9th Infantry Regiment take cover during a firefight with NVA/VC troops in Cholon.

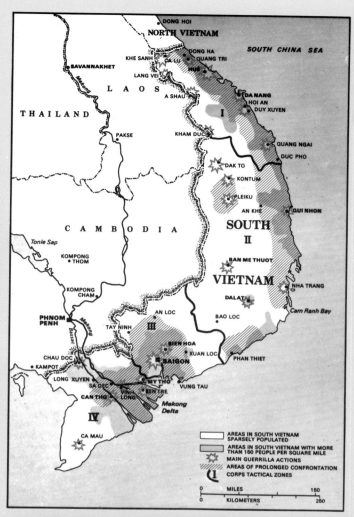

to support Khe Sanh.

In Saigon, and elsewhere in the country, the attacks began at 0300 hours on 30 January, launched by more than 5000 NVA/VC troops who had infiltrated the capital over the past weeks disguised as visiting celebrants for the Tet Holiday. It was never suspected that such massive numbers of enemy forces could enter the capital city without detection, and this surprise added to the success of the operation. However it was later revealed that the well-organized infiltration of men, weapons and supplies had been carried out over a period of several months and that they had entered the city in laundry trucks, disguised as vendors and even in mock funerals. It also became clear that Saigon harbored a well-organized cadre of Communist sympathizers who provided shelter and assembly points throughout the city. Not only had the NVA/VC assembled in secrecy but interrogations of prisoners later revealed that the Communists actually test fired their weapons during the celebration fireworks displays.

The attacks throughout Saigon began simultaneously. The NVA/VC were so certain of victory that many of them discarded their peasant clothing and donned their uniforms. This action more than any other demonstrates their contempt for the American and South Vietnamese forces. The initial targets of the attack were the American military police and South Vietnamese national police who patrolled the streets of Saigon. How the Communist forces succeeded in effectively eliminating most of these patrols remains a mystery, but they were obviously well-informed and

familiar with the routes taken and the patrol members themselves. Another major target was the Seventh Air Force Command Post at Tan Son Nhut Air Base and the adjacent MACV compound. NVA/VC troops succeeded in moving to within 1000 yards of their objectives before being challenged. Fighting at Tan Son Nhut was extremely fierce and American casualties mounted quickly as well-trained NVA soldiers faced support and maintenance personnel who lacked combat experience. The fighting became so intense that General Westmoreland withdrew to his windowless command bunker and ordered his staff to draw their weapons and reinforce the defenses. At Tan Son Nhut only 20 percent of the garrison, the security guards, were armed when the assault began. All others had to be armed in the midst of the battle from the base arsenals.

Suicide squads attacked Independence Palace, the National Police Barracks, radio stations and similar targets. The headquarters of the South Vietnamese Joint Chiefs of Staff was infiltrated by troops dressed as ARVN soldiers and fighting was so desperate and confused that most of the South Vietnamese casualties were inflicted by ARVN guards, who fired wildly

at attackers and defenders as well. A commando squad of 19 NVA/VC troops attempted to take the American Embassy. Five Military Police successfully held the attackers at bay for more than five hours until several platoons of the 101st Airborne Division arrived to defeat the commandos. The 'Battle for Bunker's Bunker' (named after Ambassador Bunker) ended with 19 NVA/VC troops and five Americans dead. Two Vietnamese chauffeurs lost their lives as a result of an order to eliminate all non-American personnel within the embassy compound.

As battle raged throughout the city, NVA/VC troops in one sector held a parade, prematurely honoring themselves as the victorious liberators and calling for the people to take up arms and join them. In other areas Communist forces held mock trials and American and South Vietnamese soldiers were tried, sentenced and executed as war criminals in full view of South Vietnamese civilians to indicate contempt for and show superiority over the Americans and the

Below: Vietnam's ancient capital city of Hue was badly damaged in the battle to retake it from the NVA/VC.
Right: smoke billows from a fuel dump at Khe Sanh.

ARVN. In the afternoon President Nguyen Van Thieu declared martial law. Although the government and American command attempted to stabilize the situation, panic and confusion continued to spread and atrocities began to occur. The incident which received the most publicity is the execution of a captured Communist soldier by the chief of the South Vietnamese National Police. His action, filmed by a cameraman, was intended to show Communist troops the fate that awaited them if captured. The Americans quickly ordered a halt to such reprisals for fear of the Communist reaction against missing American troops, but they were too late. The release of the photographs produced shock in the United States. This 30-seconds of film made Americans question what was in fact going on in Southeast Asia. Questions were raised about American support of such an apparently 'barbaric' people. The American command felt it necessary to counter the effects of the execution coverage with evidence of mass butchery by the Communists whenever possible.

Within 24 hours of the initial attacks, Saigon was a burning battleground. American air support was called in and areas which were suspected of harboring large enemy concentrations were bombed. Ground combat amounted to little more than street warfare as the American and ARVN forces moved through the city in house-to-house combat. It was quickly discovered that the primary stronghold of the Communist forces was the Cholon suburb, the home of a large Chinese Buddhist community. Cholon had been the primary assembling point and refuge of the NVA/VC prior to the offensive. The Buddhist faction had long been a thorn in the side of the South Vietnamese government and the additional indictment of aiding the enemy prompted Thieu's officials to demand that Cholon and its inhabitants be destroyed.

As American and ARVN forces attempted to dislodge the Communists from Cholon the fighting grew more intense. For the next four days the suburb was systematically cleared of Communist troops but the frustration of the American troops grew as NVA/VC forces moved back into areas which had been considered secured. At the same time Tan Son Nhut Air Base was again attacked and although reinforced with combat troops the battle continued for more than 36 hours. By 5 February the Americans and ARVN were beginning to take control of the city, with the exception of Cholon. American B-52 bombers were also called in and for the first time hit targets near Saigon. Although Intelligence reports were sketchy at best, any suspected enemy troop concentrations outside the city were given priority. In one instance the B-52s struck a position less than 10 miles from the city center and although 42 bodies were found it was impossible to confirm if they were in fact enemy troops or civilians.

As the American command was beginning to consider the situation stabilized NVA/VC forces launched a counteroffensive from Cholon on 18 February. Casualties were again high in the military and national police and Tan Son Nhut Air Base received its final assault. However conditions now favored the Americans and the counterassault was swiftly blunted. By 23 February Cholon had been 'pacified' and although skirmishing in the suburbs of Saigon continued for several weeks the Tet Offensive in the capital had been dispersed. It was later estimated that at least three NVA divisions had participated in the offensive and although it was suspected that they had not left the Saigon area they did not attempt to attack the city again. Rather than pursue the battle, American and South Vietnamese forces concentrated their efforts on restoring order and on rebuilding projects within the city itself.

The battle for the second primary target of the Tet Offensive was an even more intense struggle for American forces. The battle for Hue was launched at exactly the same time but in contrast to Saigon all major military and political objectives fell within the first few hours. Only the American advisor headquarters and the headquarters of the ARVN 3rd Division remained secure. By nightfall of the first day the NVA/VC had freed some 2500 military and political prisoners and had raised their flag over the Citadel of Hue. As NVA/VC forces took possession of communications installations in Hue they broadcast messages urging the people of South Vietnam to rise up and assist the liberation effort. In Hue the largest number of supporters joined the Communist effort, primarily from the ranks of students and professors of the university. The bulk of the civilian population was engaged in fleeing the city.

In the late afternoon of 30 January American marines and ARVN forces fought their way through the city to the advisor headquarters, freeing the advisors, then retreating from the city. Over the next few days American reinforcements joined these forces and began plans to recapture Hue. The delay in assembling an assault force of sufficient size was largely due to the commitment of troops to Khe

Sanh's defense and the assaults of NVA/VC forces on other important locations in the northern provinces. As Lieutenant General Lam (I Corps ARVN commander) and Lieutenant General Robert Cushman (marine commander of I Corps) formulated plans for the recapture of Hue they faced an unusual dilemma. Hue was the ancient capital of Vietnam and as such was the site of many historic and religious landmarks. The city was considered almost sacred by the people of South Vietnam, particularly the Buddhists who had several important religious shrines in the city. As the Buddhists were already dissenters, it would not have been prudent to give them further cause for grievance against the Americans or South Vietnamese. Therefore ground forces were used to counterattack as they would be the most effective and least destructive. It was soon discovered that the Communists had such a tight grip on the city that such 'kid glove' tactics would have to be abandoned.

During the first week of fighting whenever ground troops encountered staunch resistance, artillery and air strikes were called for support. Sectors of Hue were reduced to rubble, which itself provided cover for the NVA/VC forces. Casualties mounted rapidly as American and ARVN forces slowly inched their way through the city toward the Citadel. As they finally approached it, the Communist forces destroyed the bridge which crossed the Perfume River and linked the Citadel with the rest of Hue. Even without this, the Citadel was a commanding fortification. There was little hope of reducing the 20-foot high, 14-foot deep walls of the Citadel with air strikes or artillery. An infantry assault was launched. It was a monumental task.

In the meantime fighting continued to rage throughout the city. From 11–15 February, marines and ARVN soldiers attempted to secure what was left of the city. It was a period of intense fighting, made worse by the large numbers of casualties pinned beneath the rubble and by the army of rats which had entered the city. News correspondents reported that the situation defied description. Finally after several days of attempting to cross the Perfume River marines, supported by assault helicopters and fighter jets, successfully crossed to the Citadel and surrounded it. On 20 February the marines attacked the Citadel with ARVN troops in support. Napalm and even antipersonnel gasses were used against the defenders but it was not until 21 February that the weather cleared and fighter aircraft were able fully to support the operation. From this point on the American counteroffensive moved swiftly. By 22 February the Communist forces held only one small sector of the Citadel, and within 24 hours that position was also taken. With the Citadel lost the NVA/VC troops began to withdraw from the city and on 25 February Hue was described as secure.

Throughout the remainder of February and into the first half of March American and ARVN forces, as well as other allied troops, continued to reestablish

control in South Vietnam. Casualties during the Tet Offensive were enormous, though great discrepancies existed between American and North Vietnamese loss figures. In Hue alone the Communists claimed to have killed more than 1000 Americans and 1200 South Vietnamese troops. American figures showed 119 American and 363 ARVN lost. It is difficult to determine which figures are more accurate. But the Tet Offensive had several irrefutable consequences.

The South Vietnamese government was faced with the grim reality of some 750,000 refugees, made homeless by the combined NVA/VC and American destruction of major populated areas. Their plight necessitated rebuilding large segments of the cities and reestablishing rural communities. The strength and determination of the guerrilla and NVA forces in Vietnam was realized. The ferocity and magnitude of their offensive had taken the United States by surprise and produced long-term effects which would prove fatal to the American war effort. It highlighted the fact that American military strength in the Far East, as emphasized by the Pueblo incident in late 1967, was being stretched to its limits. Most importantly the American people were becoming more insistent on a swift end to American involvement in Vietnam. Although failing health was listed as the cause, the Tet Offensive was the major reason for President Johnson withdrawing his candidacy for reelection. A definite shift in American policy would accompany the new administration.

The Tet Offensive was not without great cost to the Communists. Although the offensive had been

Above left: men of the 9th Infantry Division fight south of the 'Y' bridge in Saigon.

Below: supplies are unloaded from a Lockheed C-130 Hercules tactical transport aircraft.

repulsed, their most devastating blow was that the people of the South failed to rally to their cause. This gave Thieu's government reason to claim that the people supported the course being followed by his government and the Americans. However Giap succeeded to some extent. Tet served to increase American awareness of the cost of the war and of the questionable methods being employed to achieve the goals. As such, Tet was in fact the foundation of the American withdrawal from Vietnam.

The confrontation at Khe Sanh continued during the Tet Offensive. Although a massive assault to overrun the base was anticipated it never materialized. As the Communists continued their bombardment and siege the marine field commander encircled his fortification with seismic sensors. Some 250 sensors

were surreptitiously placed around Khe Sanh over a 10-day period and acoustic sensors were also laid. These devices made it possible for the marines not only to plot the movement and concentration of NVA/VC forces but to actually eavesdrop on their conversations. As a result the marines were fore-warned of an enemy troop concentration at Hill 881 and of the plan for an attack on the base, which was to begin on 5 February. A massive barrage was launched against the hill but the sensors had been misleading. In fact the troops assembling around Hill 881 were massing for an attack on Hill 861A, adjacent to 881. The attack on Hill 861A caught the marines tem-porarily off guard and NVA/VC forces were on the verge of overrunning the position. When the error was realized, support artillery focussed its attention

Left: USAF security police
fight to repel an attack on Tan
Son Nhut air base.
Above: UH-1 'Huey' helicopters
were widely used as troop
transports in Vietnam. Hueys
of the 1st Air Cavalry Division
(Airmobile) are pictured.

on the attackers. The fighting for the hill was fierce as the NVA/VC had pierced the perimeters and the marines were forced into hand-to-hand combat. Finally the weight of support fire forced the Communist forces back and by the morning of 6 February both Hill 881, whose diversionary assault had been dispersed by the original artillery barrage, and Hill 861A were secured.

Sporadic fighting continued in the area until 7 February when the special forces at Lang Vei were attacked by a strong NVA/VC force supported by nearly a dozen light amphibious tanks. The assault began as night fell and although the special forces personnel and the Montagnards and Laotian Royal Army forces made a desperate attempt to defend the base they had no support equipment capable of deal-

ing with the tanks. The commander at Lang Vei requested support from Khe Sanh but the marine commander considered it to be too costly to provide helicopter and ground support to a 'hot' site at night. The base at Lang Vei was evidently about to fall so the Special Forces CO, Captain Willoughby, radioed for an artillery barrage, giving the exact coordinates of his compound. This was common practice when the situation became so desperate that no hope remained of defending a position. He then ordered his men to disperse and attempt to reach Khe Sanh or any other friendly base. Of the 24 Green Berets, 900 Montagnards and a large though unrecorded number of Laotian forces at Lang Vei, only Captain Willoughby, 13 of his men and 60 Montagnards ever reached Khe Sanh.

As Lang Vei fell the NVA/VC launched yet another attack on Khe Sanh. On 8 February the assault attained almost half of their objectives before support to Khe Sanh drove the Communists back. Fighter aircraft, tanks and even B-52 bombers, some of which dropped their ordnance within 100 meters of the Khe Sanh perimeter, gave support to the defenders. It was later revealed that by 15 February more than 100,000,000 pounds of napalm had been dropped on the surrounding area. Inclement weather put a strain on support attempts after 20 February and fog, which continued until the end of the month, gave the NVA/VC enough cover to construct an elaborate tunnel, trench and bunker system around the base. American bases in the same region, including Dong

Ha, Con Thien and Camp Carroll were kept under attack by short- and long-range artillery to prevent their forces from attempting ground support of Khe Sanh. Khe Sanh was under constant artillery attack and the NVA/VC antiaircraft weapons positioned in the hills around the base effectively stopped American attempts to support the base. Cargo aircraft for resupply had to be abandoned and American helicopters, whose speed and maneuverability made them less vulnerable, took up the task of support and resupply.

In March the noose around Khe Sanh continued to tighten. On 17 March the two NVA Divisions around the base launched yet another attack. Their primary objective was the destruction of perimeter defenses and although at one point a full NVA battalion was pitted against them, the marines managed to repulse the assault. After several days of probing attacks the NVA/VC changed their tactics from infantry to artillery attack. Throughout 23 and 24 March they bombarded the base with such intensity that the marines were forced to retreat to the questionable safety of their bunkers. However, the siege had lasted much too long for the Communists. Their offensive in other areas had been halted and South Vietnam was beginning to stabilize. The Americans and ARVN were now able to send massive reinforcements to relieve Khe Sanh.

On 1 April 'Operation Pegasus' began as units of the 1st Cavalry Division (Air Mobile) were landed by helicopter 10 miles from Khe Sanh. They first joined forces with American and ARVN troops in the area to open Route 9 so that ground support and supplies could reach Khe Sanh. Within 48 hours they were moving toward the marine base itself, only hindered by the shell craters and mines which dotted the road. On 7 April the 1st Cavalry troops and their additional support forces entered Khe Sanh virtually unopposed. Although sporadic fighting would continue in the area, the 77-day siege of Khe Sanh had been broken.

The United States declared that Khe Sanh and the Tet Offensive had been an overwhelming victory. However, the cost in American lives of Khe Sanh became a sensitive issue. The marine commanders had wanted to abandon the base when the initial buildup of troops was recognized. Its primary role was observation, and the offensive would mean that monitoring the Ho Chi Minh Trail would be virtually impossible. However, General Westmoreland ordered that the base be held. It had been proven that the only time American forces could effectively deal with the enemy was when the NVA/VC could be drawn into a conventional battle during which the superior American weapons technology could be brought to bear. Westmoreland honestly believed that a victory against the Communist in a situation such as Khe Sanh would cripple the morale of the NVA/VC. Although Giap seriously underrated the fighting ability and deter-

Above: an APC moves through Saigon in the aftermath of Tet.

mination of the American soldier, and discovered that advances in military technology made another Dien Bien Phu impossible, he knew that the 'set' battle to destroy the Communist cause and war effort simply did not exist. The Tet Offensive and Khe Sanh siege had fulfilled the North's goals even if victory had not been won. For this reason the North Vietnamese government was prepared to enter into negotiations with the South Vietnamese and Americans aimed toward a settlement. By 3 May 1968 arrangements had been made to begin peace negotiations in Paris. Johnson chose to indicate American good faith by calling a halt to the bombing of the North.

As fighting continued throughout South Vietnam the primary focus of American attention was directed at the Paris Peace Negotiations. Johnson had withdrawn his candidacy as a result of Tet and after being instrumental in taking America into the war sought to end his administration by bringing peace to Southeast Asia. The peace talks did not officially open until after Richard M Nixon had taken the oath of office in January 1969. Although a resolution of the Vietnam conflict was anticipated, the negotiations had little impact on American soldiers in Vietnam. The unwillingness of any of the belligerents, including the Vietcong's National Liberation Front army, to compromise predicted a long and bitter struggle in Paris. The United States focussed most of its attention on the military concerns of Vietnam. North Vietnam was interested, as it had been since the 1950s, in the political climate of Vietnam. The National Liberation Front submitted a Ten Point Plan which it stood firmly behind as a criteria for peace. The South Vietnamese government adamantly refused to enter into any type of coalition with the Communist factions.

The peace talks produced a major change in the attitudes of American servicemen in combat zones. Positive breakthroughs in the peace talks were anticipated every day and men in or bound for Vietnam waited for word that the war was over. While death in Vietnam was an ever-present possibility, no one wanted to be the last American soldier to die.

There were other important alterations to the American war effort as the Nixon Administration took control of the war. General Westmoreland returned to the United States to take the position of Army Chief of Staff. His deputy commander, General Creighton Abrams, took command of the MACV program. Abrams had an entirely different attitude to the Vietnam situation. He discarded Westmoreland's notion that it was possible to defeat the Communists in a conventional war and focussed his attention on the ARVN as the source of ultimate victory in Vietnam. He intended to revitalize the programs to strengthen the ARVN and in effect advocated a return to the US precombat support role.

Thus Abrams began a program of 'Vietnamization.' He began by modernizing the ARVN's arms and equipment as most of its weapons were World War II models. Once arms and equipment shipments began to arrive, he launched a major campaign to change the attitudes and tactics of the ARVN. The South Vietnamese command had become defense minded and lax as a direct result of the responsibility taken by the American military. In many areas South Vietnamese officers had initiated a five-day week. Abrams expressly forbade this practice and began a program to promote some 6000 enlisted ARVN troops to officer ranks. He also put a halt to the reconnaissance in force concept and advocated a 'hit and run' policy for ground combat against enemy positions and concentrations. Unfortunately, though useful when properly applied, the tangle of Intelligence information made it virtually impossible accurately to assess enemy strengths for such missions.

Secretary of Defense Clark Clifford, who replaced McNamara, was in full agreement with Abrams' policy. The proposed plan had three primary goals: to escalate the Vietnamization program; to speed up the peace talks; and to pressurize the Thieu government into introducing firm policies to increase South Vietnam's self-sufficiency.

The shift in American attitude came as a great shock to many South Vietnamese political and military officials. Many viewed it as abandonment of the South Vietnamese cause. Few understood it. 'Vietnamization' was primarily an attempt to fortify the South Vietnamese government and military to enable both to stand on their own strength and merit. For the United States it was a means to end military involvement in Vietnam. For American servicemen it meant less direct combat involvement in the war in most sectors of South Vietnam. As the Vietnamization program got under way it became apparent that it was an impossible dream. The United States was merely going through the motions so that it could get out of a situation which threatened to create chaos in

Above: President Nixon and Henry Kissinger, his National Security Advisor, talk to Admiral John McCain.

American society.

By 1969 the North Vietnamese and Vietcong were employing new strategies in Vietnam. A great deal of effort was put into legitimizing their political positions. The National Liberation Front of the Vietcong had formed a provisional government in the South which sought 'peaceful' recognition and support in opposition to the Thieu government. The North Vietnamese and Vietcong both widely publicized combat actions and emphasized the continuing loss of American lives. On 25 July 1969 President Nixon revealed his 'Nixon Doctrine.' He emphasized the Vietnamization program and announced that in future there would be a reduction of military and economic aid to South Vietnam. The subject of American troops withdrawals was broached but most importantly his government admitted that the United States would make every effort to stop another situation like Vietnam from ever developing. This statement amounted to an admission of the failure of past foreign policies and a shift in the direction of future American foreign policy. After the release of these statements the NVA/VC devoted even more effort to the political aspects of the Vietnam issues, returning to guerrilla warfare tactics.

As the autumn of 1969 approached several significant incidents occurred. American troop withdrawals were announced and begun. Strangely enough, the first area relinquished to the ARVN was the Mekong Delta region, traditionally a Communist area of influence. It was an obvious effort to minimize American losses by removing US troops from direct contact with enemy concentrations. NVA infiltration into the South also climbed to a startlingly high figure, though no major attacks or offensives were anticipated. In September Ho Chi Minh died after a period of deteriorating health. He would in a sense become more powerful than he had been in life as the Communist factions would strive to realize his ambition of a unified Vietnam.

6 VIETNAMIZATION

With the introduction of the Nixon Doctrine and the policies being followed by the new Administration in Washington the new decade was greeted with tension as well as hope. One of the new Vietnam programs was the reintroduction of the lottery draft system. The 'peace tomorrow' psychology still applied and the altered draft system changed the attitudes of the young men who faced military duty in Vietnam.

As the Nixon administration sought to achieve its goals of Vietnamization and American troop withdrawals, a major dilemma arose. The neighboring country of Cambodia suddenly became a source of concern. For the two years following the Tet Offensive and particularly since the Paris Peace Talks opened and American and Communist strategy changed, the NVA/VC had used Cambodia as a primary operations center. The infiltration of troops and supplies across the border had magnified the concern about the time needed for the ARVN to take control of the situation and their ability to withstand the added burden Cambodia represented. The situation became critical and, although the United States had sent massive financial aid to Cambodia to promote pro-Western attitudes, something more had to be done to throw the Communists off balance.

As the military command monitored the Communist activity in Cambodia the administration decided that the best course would be an offensive. An estimated two NVA divisions and a primary operations headquarters were close to the border with South Vietnam. There was also evidence that stockpiles of arms, equipment, food and other supplies, enough to last the Communists for almost two years, were to be found in the same area. On 1 May 1970, after careful consideration and planning, the Cambodian incursion began. The assault was preceded by heavy bombing of the region by B-52 aircraft. There were three primary objectives: the Fish Hook, the Parrot's Beak, and the Bulge areas of the Cambodian border. As American ground forces advanced, anticipating staunch Communist resistance, they were surprised to discover that their enemy had apparently fled. The first combat occurred on 3 May, but the Communists seemed unwilling to stand and fight and the action was little more than a skirmish. On 5 May American forces near Snoul again encountered a concentration of NVA troops, but aircraft supporting the drive quickly dispersed that force.

Only seven days after beginning their operation, American forces in the Fish Hook sector just south of Snoul were rewarded by the discovery of a major Communist encampment known as 'The City.' 'The City' comprised miles of interlocking tunnels and trenches and some 300 bunkers and more than 500 camouflaged huts. As 'The City' had been deserted by the Communists the American forces initially believed that any supplies or equipment which had been stored at the site had already been removed. Amazingly this was not the case and the American command was convinced that it had in fact located the primary NVA/VC military and political headquarters, Central Office for South Vietnam (COSVN). When the search of 'The City' was finally complete at least 1000 infantry weapons, 100 machine guns, some 1,000,000 rounds of ammunition and 20 tons of explosives had been uncovered. The American command was jubilant over the discovery and the consequences that the elimination of such a site would have on the Communist efforts in Cambodia. The

Below: a crew member of a USAF rescue helicopter fires his 7.62mm minigun, which was used to suppress enemy groundfire.

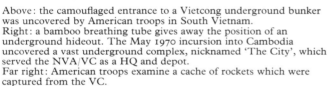

Above: the camouflaged entrance to a Vietcong underground bunker was uncovered by American troops in South Vietnam.
Right: a bamboo breathing tube gives away the position of an underground hideout. The May 1970 incursion into Cambodia uncovered a vast underground complex, nicknamed 'The City', which served the NVA/VC as a HQ and depot.
Far right: American troops examine a cache of rockets which were captured from the VC.

South Vietnamese government however was quick to react, denying that the discovery had been anything more than a large depot. In view of the South Vietnamese fears regarding the reduction of American support, such a reaction was natural. If the Americans had indeed eliminated the primary enemy operational headquarters in Cambodia then there would be little cause to continue the incursion. The Saigon government was anxious for the Americans to continue their drive until NVA/VC forces in Cambodia were encountered and destroyed, regardless of the cost in American lives.

As the Fish Hook operation continued, yet another drive by American and ARVN forces began on 4 May. The offensive was directed at the Se Sam Valley region and supported other operations in the Parrot's Beak. Although neither this advance nor the one staged at the Bulge had the same success as the Fish Hook operations, Communist forces were encountered and with successful results. Operations involving American forces continued until 29 June with

ARVN forces continuing their campaign until August. However as early as 3 June the American command and President Nixon himself issued statements which proclaimed an overwhelming victory in the American war effort and a successful step toward American withdrawal from Vietnam.

The incursion, or invasion as some chose to term it, into Cambodia resulted in several positive effects. It caused a major setback to the functioning of the NVA/VC in the entire region. Intelligence reports estimated that between one third and one half of all Communist weapons and supplies in Cambodia had been captured or destroyed. More than 3000 enemy casualties were sustained, with higher figures quoted as a result of the presumed losses incurred by the enemy during the initial bombing raids. The United States claimed that the success of the ARVN forces during and after the Americans participated in the offensive was a clear illustration of the success of the Vietnamization program.

However the Cambodian incursion had a great

many adverse effects and caused widespread reaction around the world. It made the already unstable government of Cambodia even less eager to support the pro-West faction. The aid which the American government had promised had begun to flow less readily with the administration's efforts to disengage from the war. The offensive produced a loud outcry from the Communist elements within Cambodia and threatened a further shift in the power structure. Militarily the American effort successfully eliminated much of the Communists' supplies, but the commanders and the majority of troops which the NVA/VC had positioned in Cambodia had evaded the Americans and had simply drifted further into the countryside, able and willing to begin their operations once again. When the ARVN and the Americans were unwilling or unable to remain in the areas that they had allegedly pacified the Communists simply returned to reestablish their power base.

Perhaps the worst result of the Cambodian operation was the response it received in the United States and from American allies around the world. Regardless of the justifiable reasons which could be given for the offensive, the American people saw the incursion as nothing more than an escalation of the war. Nixon had promised to get the country out of Vietnam and it appeared as though he merely intended to exchange one war zone for another. The outcry in America proved to the Communists that the United States would be forced to leave Southeast Asia in the not too distant future. Congress had acted to extricate the country from its commitment. While American forces were still engaged in the final phases of the Cambodian operation Congress repealed the Southeast Asian/Gulf of Tonkin Resolution on 24 June 1970. Studies of the situation had revealed that even with continued direct American involvement in the war it could take another decade or more of serious commitment before the United States could claim a victory in Vietnam. The general consensus was that in spite of the prolonged commitment once America ended support of the South Vietnamese government, it would collapse. The immediate effect of the resolution's repeal was to end American military responsibility to protect South Vietnam – a complete reversal of past American policy.

Throughout the remainder of 1970 both the United States and the Communist factions continued to follow the new strategies which had been set. Although combat continued, the Nixon administration made every effort to publicize the positive aspects of the American disengagement and the progress being made toward Vietnamization. One particular attempt was made to bolster American morale in the United States and cast the Nixon administration in a favorable light. On 21 November American Special Forces commandos implemented a raid into North Vietnam which was intended to free American prisoners of war

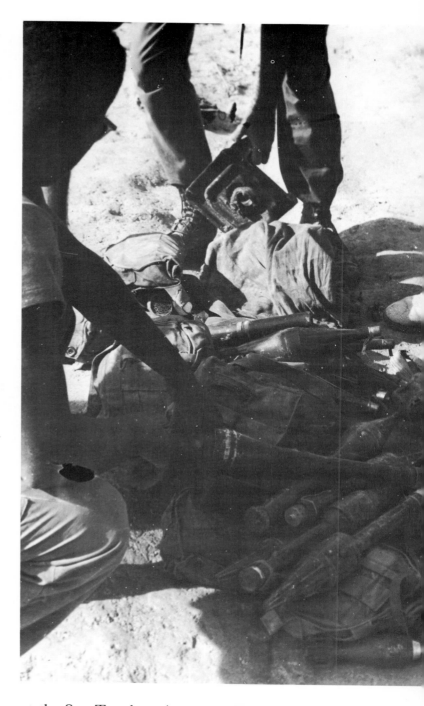

at the Son Tay detention camp. The assault, which took place less than 23 miles from Hanoi, was well organized and expertly executed. The only problem was that the prisoners were no longer being held at Son Tay. It was not merely an unlucky circumstance. The results of the raid clearly illustrated the lack of cooperation between various agencies within the Intelligence community. For some time an operation had been underway which seeded the clouds in the area. This produced unnatural rainfall and the resulting floods forced the abandonment of Son Tay shortly before the commando raid occurred.

The final months of 1970 were uncomfortably quiet for the bulk of American ground troops. Their offen-

sive commitments had been curtailed, leaving the primary combat role to the air force. Yet it was widely acknowledged that the Communists were strengthening their positions throughout Southeast Asia. The troop buildups in South Vietnam were particularly marked in the I Corps provinces and the Central Highlands, but there were large numbers of NVA/VC forces in the DMZ and the Ho Chi Minh Trail region of Laos. In fact although the Communists were consolidating their forces they were playing a relatively quiet waiting game, gathering strength for the day when the Americans would leave South Vietnam. During this period the South Vietnamese expressed their anger with the Americans. They were well aware that the United States intended to withdraw from their country. After the years of war there were many who were not sorry to see the Americans leave, but at the same time they dreaded the consequences of being left alone to cope with their own government and the North Vietnamese and Vietcong.

While the country remained comparatively quiet 1971 brought plans for yet another operation to confound Communist aggression against the South. In Da Nang American and South Vietnamese commanders were formulating a two-phase offensive against the Communists in Laos. The American operation, which was officially restricted to support activities and was to remain within South Vietnam, was known as Operation Dewey Canyon II. The ARVN phase was given the code name Lam Son (total victory) 719. The primary objectives of the assault were to sever the Ho Chi Minh Trail and to drive into Laos to Tchepone and destroy the large quantities of Communist supplies and materiel which were believed to be stockpiled in the region. Since the successful operations in Cambodia, Laos had taken a new, more dangerous part in the Communist offensive strategy and it was considered essential that its role be eliminated.

Lam Son 719 consisted of four interdependent stages. The first stage, scheduled to begin on 30 January, was a combined American-ARVN operation to secure Route 9 from Quang Tri to the Laotian border. The Rock Pile site was one of many fortified to protect the highway. The abandoned airfield at Khe Sanh was to be reactivated and reinforced and would prove crucial to the support of Lam Son if Route 9 should be severed by enemy forces. The second stage, to be initiated on 8 February, consisted of the ARVN advance from Khe Sanh across the Laotian border to Tchepone. It was to be a mechanized assault combined with helicopter support to secure the surrounding countryside and advance as rapidly as possible toward its objective. The third stage was to begin two days later and was scheduled to continue for approximately one month, during which time the ARVN was to establish a firm control over the area between the border and Tchepone. This critical phase of the

Left: an infantry patrol returns to its fire support base at the end of a search-and-clear mission.

Above: ARVN machine gunners man their foxhole. The fighting qualities of the ARVN were severely tested by Vietnamization.

offensive had the purpose of destroying Communist supplies and operations in the region and establishing fire support bases from which to conduct missions around Tchepone and the Ho Chi Minh Trail. The fourth and final stage was the withdrawal, which was to begin on 10 March.

As preparations were being made General Lam, ARVN commander of I Corps, assigned the Lam Son offensive to the 1st ARVN Infantry Division. These troops had received massive consignments of modern arms and equipment as well as specialized training and instruction. General Lam considered the 1st ARVN Division the elite troops of his command and Lam intended to demonstrate that the ARVN could function effectively without American combat forces 'holding their hands.' He would thus prove that Vietnamization of the war effort was functioning properly. The 1st ARVN Division was supported by the 1st ARVN Armor Brigade and the elite ARVN Rangers. Three battalions of Rangers were to participate in the offensive. Although they retained their American advisors this was to be a strictly ARVN operation and the advisors were to remain discreetly in the background. Reserve forces for the offensive

would consist of the South Vietnamese Marines and the elite ARVN Airborne Division. These Airborne forces had long been held as their country's reserve and were stationed in and around Saigon. However in the past their primary function had been to demonstrate strength and support for the South Vietnamese government and quelling rebellion among the Buddhists in Saigon. Their character as a fighting unit was feared and despised by much of the civilian and military population and, although they held a position of favor, their fighting ability was questionable. American advisors particularly did not trust the Airborne Division. There had been various accounts of the airborne forces terrorizing local civilians and it was feared that at some point there might be a clash between American and airborne forces. In short, their inclusion in the Lam Son venture met with disapproval from many quarters.

General Sutherland, commander of I Corps and his own XXIV Corps, mobilized his forces for the operation. XXIV Corps, which was to participate in the support of Lam Son 719, was the largest single

corps in Southeast Asia and its forces were considered able veterans. The American phase would involve some 10,000 troops, 2000 aircraft and 600 helicopters. Included in these numbers would be members of General Sutherland's personal staff and advisors, a unit of engineers, a battalion of military police to keep Route 9 secure, two brigades of airborne infantry from the 101st Airborne Division, a full combat aviation battalion, the 11th Brigade of the 23rd Infantry Division, the 1st Brigade of the 5th Infantry Division (Mechanized), and XXIV Corps' Artillery Group.

The Lam Son 719 operation was anticipated as a repetition of the incursion into Cambodia. South Vietnamese commanders were convinced that once the campaign began the NVA/VA would withdraw as they had done less than a year before. Although advisors warned that the proximity of Laos to North Vietnam would naturally mean greater resistance, it was believed that the strength of American support and air superiority would adequately reinforce the South Vietnamese operations. The Intelligence

Above left: a 105mm howitzer of the 6th Battalion, 11th Artillery Regiment, pictured in action at fire-support base 'Charlie 2' in March 1971.
Above: troops leap from a UH-1 to set up a defensive perimeter, while the helicopter's gunner prepares to lend support.

gathered and supplied for the operation was inconclusive. There were reports that enemy tanks had been spotted, but as there had been little surveillance on the ground, the combined commands relied on aerial photography for their information. Most important was the report that an aircraft carrying members of General Lam's staff had been shot down in western Quang Tri Province. Although the South Vietnamese command refused to corroborate the claim, it should have been considered that there was at least a possibility that it was true and that the enemy forces might have captured the battle plans.

The most crucial shortcoming in the organization of Intelligence was that MACV Headquarters was orchestrating the operation and refused to give adequate consideration to the Intelligence-gathering sources of I Corps itself. All details of enemy troop concentrations were compiled and released through MACV Headquarters. Although this system works well at a strategic level, it ignores the firsthand knowledge and intuition of those who work in the field of operation on a daily basis. The alleged infallibility of the highly-classified MACV Intelligence overrode the information supplied by smaller field units and this proved to be disastrous.

A news media blackout preceded the advance of the 5th Mechanized Division toward Khe Sanh on 30 January 1971, ordered by General Sutherland as it had been repeatedly proven that American journalists could publicize military operations before the North could gather Intelligence on its own. Three battalions of the 101st Airborne Division landed by helicopter at the abandoned Khe Sanh airfield and, as units of those battalions worked to bring the airfield into operation, other units advanced to secure Lang Vei. This was crucial as American personnel were to advance no further than this old special forces camp.

The initial phase of the campaign proceeded much

more easily than had been anticipated. The Khe Sanh site was discovered to be in relatively good condition, requiring little more than minor restoration and repair. By the morning of 1 February leading elements of the ARVN advance had already penetrated the border of Laos. While the situation appeared to be progressing well in Vietnam, around the world the United States was being subjected to open hostility from friends and enemies alike. From Moscow came accusations of 'Capitalistic, imperialistic aggression,' while allies in Europe and the Secretary General of the United Nations expressed their disapproval of escalating the war and carrying it beyond the boundaries of South Vietnam once again. In the United States this offensive so soon after the Cambodian affair produced a vociferous outcry from antiwar activists and congressmen, led by Senator Mike Mansfield, condemned the Nixon administration for reneging on its promises to end the war.

As planned the second phase of Lam Son 719 began on 8 February as the 1st Infantry Division, 1st Armor Brigade and Rangers of the ARVN moved from Route 9 across the Laotian border, severing the Ho Chi Minh Trail and commencing their advance on Tchepone. As they advanced they established fire support bases. Within 24 hours the army brigade had traversed half the distance to Tchepone. The only significant problems were a result of poor weather conditions and it appeared as if the offensive would achieve its goals. But the NVA/VC were neither fleeing nor standing idly by. The entire operation was being carefully monitored to gauge the true nature of the offensive. Apparently the North Vietnamese command thought that the invasion of Laos by the ARVN could be a diversionary tactic to draw attention from a major American assault on the DMZ region. When it was finally decided that Laos was the real target, the NVA 70B Corps prepared to counter the ARVN offensive.

ARVN forces began to encounter earnest resistance, primarily in the form of ambushes against mechanized units and assaults on the newly established support bases. By 12 February NVA forces had begun to bring pressure to bear against Dong Ha, the junction point of supplies moving toward Khe Sanh along Route 9. The resistance intensified and although the South Vietnamese government announced that the Ho Chi Minh Trail had been severed it was obvious that Communist supplies were still moving South. During the following week the ARVN advance came to a complete halt but rather than admit that the offensive was encountering major difficulties the South Vietnamese government announced that the advance had penetrated Laos far enough. On 23

Left: UH-1 'Hueys' return to Bu Dop camp to refuel at the end of a mission. An escorting AH-1 Hueycobra helicopter gunship brings up the rear.

February President Thieu proclaimed Lam Son 719 an overwhelming victory.

Less than 24 hours before that announcement Ranger Base South in Laos was completely surrounded. The ARVN sister base Ranger Base North had been encircled by NVA antiaircraft artillery which effectively prevented aerial resupply or reinforcement. The bases faced imminent capture and the ARVN rangers were ordered to evacuate. The ARVN forces received more than 300 casualties, though they claimed to have killed some 600 NVA troops. On 25 February 2000 NVA soldiers supported by at least 20 light tanks attacked the support base known as Airborne Objective 31. Some 500 of the elite airborne forces defended the base against numerous assaults, giving a good account of themselves. However, by 28 February they were forced to abandon the site and attempted to rendezvous with other ARVN forces on Route 9. Of their number 120 were listed as casualties or captured, including the battalion commander.

By 1 March the northern flank of the spearhead into Laos had begun to collapse. The situation was becoming critical for the ARVN. Three full NVA divisions were maneuvering along the northern front and, with American close air support hampered by bad weather, General Lam realized that he must salvage the Lam Son operation as best he could. Tchepone was out of reach of the ground forces and General Lam focussed his forces to counter the threat of the NVA divisions. On 5 March the 1st ARVN Infantry Division was airlifted by American helicopters to establish three primary Landing Zones (LZs) along the northern perimeter of the invasion sector. The following day clear weather permitted an aerial attack by B-52 bombers on Tchepone. This paved the way for the American airlift of two ARVN infantry battalions to a point approximately four miles outside Tchepone. Although they took Tchepone, it was deserted and the enemy supplies removed. The ARVN were thus denied a major victory. In Khe Sanh on 8 March an official press release claimed that Lam Son had been a great success, achieving its two primary objectives of creating chaos for the Communist in Laos and restricting the flow of supplies along the Ho Chi Minh Trail.

On 10 March according to the original battle plans ARVN troops were ordered to withdraw from Laos. General Lam anticipated a massive Communist counteroffensive to coincide with the arrival of the April rainy season. The majority of his troops were already seriously occupied with enemy forces. Two days later the NVA proved that General Lam had underestimated their preparedness – the counteroffensive began. The American support personnel were now taxed to their limits to keep the NVA offensive from converting a withdrawal into a rout. From 13–18 March a running battle ensued as American helicopters flew missions throughout the

On 25 March American helicopter crews of the 101st Airborne Division flew the final missions over Laos for the removal of ARVN forces. Although the government in Saigon announced that all ARVN forces had been evacuated, American air crews claimed to have seen many pockets of ARVN forces attempting to fight their way to the established landing zones but such reports were disclaimed as a great victory was announced. It was claimed that the ARVN lost only 6000 dead, wounded or missing during the operation and that some 12,000 casualties had been inflicted on the NVA. Hanoi similarly claimed victory, stating that more than 15,000 ARVN and 200 American troops had been killed, wounded or captured. Although it is impossible to confirm the actual troop losses it can be estimated that approximately 50 percent of the ARVN which entered Laos could be classified as casualties. American casualties, equally difficult to estimate as no official figures are given, were at least 25.

Technically the Lam Son 719 operation could be classified as a failure. It was far removed from the success that had been achieved in Cambodia and, although the South Vietnamese command inflated figures of captured enemy supplies and equipment and casualties inflicted, it was obvious by the continued advance of NVA forces that no serious damage had been done to their operational capabilities. Most important was the effect Lam Son had on the claims of progress in the Vietnamization program. Not only did it prove that the ARVN alone was no match for the NVA/VC, but those who died in Laos were South Vietnam's best troops. The South Vietnamese government and military had overestimated the ability of its forces and underestimated the Communists. It was evident that the ARVN still needed American forces to manage situations which the South Vietnamese government and military had allowed to get out of control. Regardless of the claims of victory, Lam Son was a devastating blow to the morale of the ARVN and to Nixon's claims that 'Vietnamization' would bring a swift end to American involvement in the conflict in Southeast Asia.

As American and ARVN forces reconsolidated and reorganized after the offensive the NVA/VC increased activity along the DMZ and throughout the northern provinces and the central highlands. It became increasingly difficult for American forces to hold outlying fire support bases and maintain the low profile which had been ordered to minimize losses. By the end of April Khe Sanh had once more been abandoned and by 1 July many of the fire support bases in the highly active sectors were evacuated. Bombing again became the primary means of attacking the enemy. The Ho Chi Minh Trail was the target of heavy bombing raids and although increased air strikes were mounted they were becoming more dangerous in the face of antiaircraft, surface-to-air

operation zone to retrieve ARVN forces. Although their orders stated simply, 'Get as many ARVN out as you can,' pilots seldom knew if the landing zone they approached was held by ARVN or NVA troops. The panic and confusion of the evacuation was reported worldwide, though for the most part the chaos in Laos was seen only by American relief personnel. In their fear of capture by enemy forces ARVN troops swarmed the arriving Huey helicopters. Hueys were designed to carry eight to 12 men but often so many ARVN troops climbed aboard that their weight prevented the Hueys from becoming airborne. The courage of American air crews throughout the evacuation displayed the finest qualities of American armed forces.

What is considered the last major battle between ARVN and NVA forces occurred on 22 March at Fire Base Alpha, where ARVN marines fought desperately for more than four hours. When it became evident that the NVA troops were going to overrun the base, American helicopters again flew missions to extract the South Vietnamese soldiers. As on so many other occasions during the withdrawal, ARVN forces swarmed the helicopters, confirming to the watching NVA troops that without the Americans to support them the ARVN were an undisciplined rabble.

missiles and the MiG-21 fighter aircraft being employed. In October Thieu was reelected President, which did little to quiet the discontent of the population who were growing tired of his methods. The second half of 1971 again saw the NVA/VC build their strength and solidify their hold over various sectors of the South in anticipation of the American withdrawal from Southeast Asia. By the end of the year the United States' troop commitment had fallen to 139,000, less than half of what it had been only one year earlier. The South Koreans, Australians and New Zealanders were also rapidly leaving the country. It was clear that few cared if the Vietnamization program was operating properly or not, they simply wanted to rid themselves of an unpleasant, unpopular situation. Soon the ARVN would be forced to stand alone and face what had been delayed for over 15 years – direct confrontation without outside help.

With the arrival of 1972 old problems with new meaning were again brought into focus. Both the American and South Vietnamese military leaders recognized the signs that the Communists were preparing yet another major offensive. It was apparent that they were merely waiting for more American troops to be withdrawn before pressing their advantage. During the first three months of 1972 the NVA/VC forces grew bolder and made more attacks in the Northern Provinces. The fighting was particularly heavy in the region around Hue. In the south there was an ominous calm. Terrorist attacks with Soviet-made rockets were the only reminder in some areas that the war was still going on. NVA/VC operations were mostly aimed at disrupting government programs in the South. The South Vietnamese were now certain that the Americans, who had failed to bring them peace, were deserting them. The Communists took every opportunity to dwell upon the failings of both the government in the South and the Americans. Although the NVA/VC had not won any major military victories they were rapidly gaining ground. In spite of American military and, more importantly, political efforts to stabilize the situation South Vietnam was on the brink of chaos.

The Communists believed that they had their enemies 'on the run' and the time seemed perfect for

Left: President Richard M Nixon talks to troops of the US 1st Infantry Division during his tour of South Vietnam.

Below: a US Army CH-47 Chinook heavy-lift helicopter flies supplies to a hilltop fire-support base.

another offensive. The American and ARVN forces had attempted to dominate the situation with their invasions of Cambodia and Laos during the past two years. The NVA/VC believed that a successful offensive would help speed the Americans on their way and would show the weaknesses of the South Vietnamese government. The Communist offensive began on 30 March 1972, only one week after the Paris Peace Talks resumed. It consisted of four primary fronts. The first was to drive directly across the DMZ and along the main coastal highway, Route 1, with American and ARVN military installations at Dong Ha and Quang Tri as primary targets. An additional phase of this front included an attack on the A Shau Valley to eliminate American fire support bases, then swing to rejoin the thrust from the North to capture Hue, and thus take control of the two northernmost provinces. The second front was directed against Binh Dinh Province, which bordered Cambodia, with the objective of capturing the provincial capital and taking a firm grasp of Route 13, a major highway which ran directly into Saigon. The Communists anticipated great success on this front as anti-American and South Vietnamese government feelings were strong after the Cambodian incursion. The objective on the third front was to capture Kontum and Routes 19 and 14 which linked the Central Highlands with the coastal regions. Finally, a major effort was to be directed against the military boundary between I Corps and II Corps to isolate the five northern provinces from the rest of South Vietnam.

At first the NVA/VC enjoyed success on all fronts. In all but a few areas the ARVN offered little resistance, immediately withdrawing to fortified American bases. Bad weather prevented American aircraft from fully supporting the ARVN. Although some 15,000 NVA troops and over 200 Soviet-built tanks were temporarily stalled along the Qua Viet River in Quang Tri Province, by 9 April they had crossed the river at three primary points. Dong Ha fell and both American and ARVN forces struggled to reinforce and hold the province. One month after the Communist offensive began the Nixon Administration decided that conditions in the northern provinces had become too volatile to permit American troops and advisors to remain. This decision was to have far-reaching consequences. As it seemed that the NVA/VC would ultimately take control of the provinces, the administration wanted American personnel removed before it could become another disaster. US helicopters began urgent evacuation of American troops and General Vu Giai, commander of ARVN forces in that sector, demanded that he and his staff also be removed. By the night of 1 May word had spread throughout the ARVN ranks that the Americans and their commander had fled. This proved that the Americans had no faith in the ARVN's ability to contain the Communist advance

and that the Americans did not intend to expend lives in a futile defense. The majority of American support personnel were withdrawn a 'safe' distance away from the most active combat zones.

Panic spread rapidly through the ARVN units in Quang Tri Province, who fled to Hue. Elsewhere the situation was only slightly less severe. At An Loc in Binh Dinh Province ARVN forces held the Communist advance using American M-72 antitank missiles. American B-52s played a crucial role, bombing NVA/VC concentrations and supply routes in Binh Dinh and Cambodia. In the area around Kontum mechanized NVA/VC forces from Cambodia and Laos quickly overwhelmed the ARVN positions. Although American air support gave assistance whenever possible, ARVN and South Korean forces were virtually trapped in Kontum. The final phase of the NVA/VC offensive began on 14 April. With ARVN, allied and American support overtaxed on other fronts, the division of I Corps from II Corps was easily accomplished. A large percentage of ARVN forces simply discarded their weapons and uniforms and deserted.

Although General Abrams made every attempt to convince the Nixon Administration that it was essential to commit American ground forces, his requests were denied. The Paris Peace Talks had foundered and bombings of the North and the mining of North Vietnamese ports were intensified, but Nixon adamantly clung to his troop-withdrawal program. By June the American air war and increased naval activity had begun to take their toll. The supply of materials had been greatly reduced as air strikes destroyed supply transports and crucial bridges. The US air offensive continued to escalate until August, when more than 1000 missions were flown in three days, at least 25 percent of them against the North itself.

Near the end of June General Abrams was suddenly relieved of command. He was replaced by General Fred C Weyand, who had been involved in the peace talks. His primary function was to ensure that troop withdrawals were in accordance with Nixon's doctrine. In July the peace negotiations were resumed as ARVN forces launched a country-wide counteroffensive. By the end of September most of the ground lost in April and May had been regained. The success of the counteroffensive was undoubtedly a result of the American air war, but Communist forces persistently reorganized and reconsolidated their strength.

The offensive clearly demonstrated that the struggle was by no means over. While the incursions into Laos and Cambodia had been setbacks for the NVA/VC they could still launch a major offensive on multiple fronts which could do serious damage to the ARVN and undermine the government's position in Saigon. It also illustrated that the success attributed to 'Vietnamization' was merely America's attempt to save

Above: the pilot of a B-52 bomber shot down during an attack on Hanoi is shown to pressmen by his captors.

face and free itself from the war. Although supporters of the program claimed that the summer counteroffensive proved the ARVN to be capable fighters, critics were quick to point out that motivation was still lacking. Only a few of the most well-equipped units, whose officers were highly disciplined, could be counted on to fight without direct American combat support. The most shocking aspect for the Americans was the realization that despite everything the Communists had the will and means to continue the war.

Although massive troop withdrawals just prior to the November presidential elections had been a crucial factor in Nixon's victory, the antiwar atmosphere demanded that he bring a swift end to America's involvement in Vietnam. In the aftermath of the offensive and counteroffensive the United States searched desperately for an ally which would take up the struggle where America left off. However the Australians and New Zealanders had departed before the ARVN counteroffensive began, leaving a minimal number of advisors with explicit orders to remain strictly noncombatant. South Korea was offered considerable American support to continue its role until 'Vietnamization' was complete but it refused, removing its final 30,000 troops before the end of 1972. Thailand, which had the most to lose if South Vietnam fell, withdrew all but 100 of its support troops. With the refusal of SEATO allies to involve themselves further, the Nixon Administration saw its hopes dissolve. Added to this was the fact that in the wake of the American and ARVN incursions and the

subsequent NVA/VC success, Cambodia and Laos became solidly pro-Communist. By December 1972 American strength had officially been reduced to 25–30,000 support personnel. The end was near.

On 8 January 1973 the Paris Peace Talks resumed and for the first time it appeared that positive progress would be made. Within two weeks Nixon stopped the bombings and the framework of a peace settlement was drawn up on 23 January. The following day all belligerents initialled the tentative agreement in Paris. That afternoon representatives of all the governments announced victory in Vietnam. Official delegates of the United States, South Vietnam, North Vietnam and the People's Revolutionary Party (Vietcong) met on 27 January to sign the final peace agreement. The principal provisions of the agreement were that the United States would withdraw all troops immediately. Within 60 days all prisoners of war would be released to their respective countries. The United States was to begin mine-clearing operations in North Vietnamese harbors, particularly the port of Haiphong. A four-party joint military commission and an international commission were to be established to supervise the transitions.

MACV Headquarters ceased to operate and the last American combat advisors flew from Tan Son Nyut airfield on 15 March 1973. The war which was not officially a war was over for the United States.

7 THE AIR WAR

One of the most publicized aspects of the Vietnam conflict was the American air war. The air war was the most expedient method of retaliation against the Communists although its early stages Operation Barrel Roll and OPLAN 34 were not solely retaliatory. They were designed to demonstrate the North's vulnerability to air-strikes and to undermine the morale of the North Vietnamese armed forces and populace.

The air war was divided into two distinct components, tactical and strategic. The tactical air war encompassed missions flown in direct support of American and ARVN units. An integral phase of tactical air support was helicopter operations, which most closely affected American ground forces. The strategic air war involved attacks on known infiltra-

tion routes and the North itself.

Tactically American, South Vietnamese and SEATO ally forces received what can only be classified as the best close air support ever witnessed in combat. It was usually only a matter of minutes from the time air support was requested until it appeared. F-4 Phantoms, F-105 Thunderchiefs and Cessna A-37 Dragonfly jets, as well as less sophisticated propeller aircraft such as the Douglas A-1 Skyraider, could be counted upon to bring their ordnance to bear against the enemy. However their support capabilities led American and allied troops to rely too heavily on tactical aircraft and ground units often became overextended, depending on air support missions to save the situation.

Support helicopters such as the Huey Cobra and

Huey Gunships, which carried light machine guns, miniguns or rocket pods were particularly effective in combat. B-52 bombers were employed in tactical roles as required. As evidenced at Khe Sanh, B-52s bombed troop concentrations and enemy artillery positions which were more commonly the task of smaller ground attack aircraft. Known by the inglorious title 'Big Belly' B-52D bombers carried 40–

ground troops whose lives depended on the expertise of air crews.

Ground support given by helicopters was an equal if not superior partner in the tactical air war. The army had fought desperately to retain the helicopter against air force claims that it should fall solely under its jurisdiction. In the army's hands it became one of the most widely-used tactical weapons

Left: an F-4 Phantom of the USAF's 8th Tactical Fighter Wing releases a laser-guided bomb. These 'smart bombs' greatly increased the accuracy of American air strikes.

50 bombs internally and half as many again on underwing racks. Their missions were later given the code name 'Arc Light' as from the ground their striking ordnance resembled the flash of a welding rod on metal. Their ordnance had devastating effects. One bomber's mission could virtually destroy a half-mile square area. Few ground personnel ever survived such attacks, but those who did reported that the earth seemed to explode without warning. The lack of warning of B-52 attacks proved an effective terror tactic against the enemy.

As the need demanded the United States increased the sophistication of its weapons. Aircraft were fitted with 20mm miniguns for strafing raids, and rocket pods which held 48 free-flight rockets could saturate an area with high explosives. Various bomb types were improved and developed, ranging from high-explosive antipersonnel types to napalm and 'smart' bombs. 'Smarts,' although primarily designed for strategic targets, were occasionally employed in support of ground troops to dislodge enemy artillery positions when conventional means proved ineffective. Improved radar techniques gave ground-support aircraft the capability of delivering bombs with pinpoint accuracy. Although support ordnance could explode on friendly forces, it was most often the result of misinformation relayed from forward observers and ground controllers. Tactically the air war was 99 percent effective and greatly appreciated by

of the Vietnam era, earning the respect of the soldier and the nickname 'workhorse of the war.' The helicopter's potential was immediately recognized. Its ability to land virtually anywhere gave American forces previously unheard of mobility. The helicopter was the primary instrument in denying the guerrilla forces their freedom of the countryside, forcing them into the most inhospitable terrain. As the versatility, dependability and serviceability of the helicopter improved it became a frontline fighting machine. In combat it could deliver troops to any site, but more importantly helicopters could remove ground forces if the situation became too dangerous, whereas previously paratroopers were forced to fight their way out of adverse situations. Known as 'Dust Off' operations, helicopters could evacuate wounded troops even from inaccessible areas and get them to medical facilities in a matter of minutes, saving lives that would otherwise have been lost. The CH-47 Chinook and the UH-1 Huey were most commonly used as transport aircraft for troops on fire support bases and in the field. Finally, the ability of the helicopter to transport supplies and reinforcements to any location solved a dilemma that had faced armies for centuries. Special helicopters were designed to fill these particular roles. Quite simply, there was little the helicopter could not do. Direct ground support, troop and supply transport, reconnaissance, directing artillery and air strikes and

airborne ambulance missions were all within the helicopters capability, making it a close friend to the infantry.

The least productive aspect of the American air war was the strategic phase. Originally designed to harass the enemy through the destruction of supply routes and primary military and industrial installations in the North, a 'proving ground' mentality developed which overshadowed the true objectives. In addition to strategic bombing, ground sensors, ground-surveillance radar, surveillance aircraft and drones were geared to monitor and disrupt enemy troop and materiel infiltration. Although efforts were made through bombing to bring pressure to bear, it was a futile exercise. Occasionally enemy troops and

Top left: ARVN troops file aboard UH-1s. The helicopter gave US and ARVN forces unrivalled battlefield mobility.
Above left: a UH-1B helicopter gunship pours fire into a VC position in the Mekong Delta.
Above right: VC prisoners are loaded aboard a 'Huey.'

supply transports were caught in strategic air strikes, but more often nothing more was accomplished than the destruction of the local flora and fauna. Intelligence findings indicated that strategic bombing of supply routes had less effect on enemy movement than the monsoon rains did, but their opinions were ignored.

The strategic air war against the North became the true test site for air technology as 'superweapons'

were introduced. The United States and Soviet Union supplied sophisticated weapons systems and aircraft for trial and refinement against one another in both offensive and defensive roles. As with other aspects of the conflict in Vietnam, the situation provided wartime experience without the holocaust of actual war between the two superpowers. Perhaps the most serious blunder the United States made was the bombing of Hanoi, Haiphong and other primary North Vietnamese cities. The people of North Vietnam were not cowed by the bombings. As had been proven in the Blitz of London, Allied bombing of Germany and the raids on Tokyo, bombing tended to harden the determination of the people to resist.

The strategic air war was maintained by agencies of the US air force which believed that their service branch did not have a substantial program in Vietnam. Concerned lest the air force be passed over for funding and new military hardware by the demands of the army, a niche was created and expanded. The policy cost many American lives and was a primary source of American prisoners of war, all for a military lesson which should have been obvious to all concerned.

The American air war on a tactical level was a valuable asset to the war effort. The errors made on the strategic level created an indecisiveness in the American perspective on strategic bomber aircraft that would, unfortunately, lead to missiles being viewed as the only valid strategic weapon.

8 'PEACE WITH HONOR'

Of all the wars in which Americans have fought Vietnam was without a doubt the one in which soldiers experienced the greatest psychological difficulties. The essence of war is to neutralize the designated enemy. However Vietnam was the first occasion when American servicemen lacked full comprehension of the definition of that enemy. To understand the course of the war it is necessary to understand the men who fought in Vietnam and the pressures brought to bear on them, not only in Southeast Asia but in and from the United States.

Initially American military personnel in Southeast Asia did not have conflicting interests. Their role was advisory, to instruct the South Vietnamese military in the art of modern warfare, and few of them came into direct contact with the enemy. Thus the war had been sterilized, never personally affecting them. The first men to take an active combat role were special forces personnel who had an elite status as professional soldiers.

In the post World War II anti-Communist 'Cold War' era the United States Army developed a commando force whose purpose was to carry out surreptitious activities behind enemy lines. Although its primary objective was Eastern Europe, the organization rapidly developed into a specialized unit for commando paratroop deployment into 'hot spots' world wide. President John F Kennedy played a vital role in promoting the special forces. Known then as Green Berets, from the headgear they adopted from the British, they became Kennedy's 'superforce.' They were a means to secure the role of the United States, and the President, as the rightful defenders of the ideologies of the Free World against the growing influence of Communism in the Far East and South America.

Throughout American involvement in Vietnam more than 5000 men would serve under the classification special forces advisors, though not all were Green Berets. The operations in which they participated, their close contact with the South Vietnamese, and the mystique which surrounded special forces personnel segregated them from the mass of American servicemen in Vietnam. They were simultaneously feared, hated, admired and respected, but never completely trusted. Special forces were res-

ponsible for sensitive and classified operations of various types which ranged from Intelligence gathering to counterinsurgency. Unfortunately although the vast majority executed their roles with great distinction, and little recognition, such operations as the 1969 Phoenix Program received enormous attention. Originally designed as an Intelligence-gathering mission program, 'Phoenix' degenerated into a 'hit squad.' Its function was to neutralize Communist supporters and sympathizers. In conjunction with the Luc Luong Dac Biet (LLDB), the South Vietnamese offshoot of American special forces, the arrest, detention and execution of suspected Communist agents ran out of control. At least 80 percent of those arrested as Communist agents were not associated with the NVA/VC. Of that number at least 30 percent were executed before they could be interrogated. The resulting publicity blackened the reputation of the special forces and gave fuel to those who opposed the war. The primary difficulty encountered by special forces personnel in Vietnam was a division of loyalty. Their close association and cooperation with the civilians and certain military forces of South Vietnam gave them an appreciation of the needs of the Vietnamese people, often in conflict with the demands of the American war machine. The fact that they were ostracized by other branches of the military aggravated the situation.

As the war continued it became increasingly evident that advisory combat support was inadequate. The ARVN proved incapable of countering the Communist threat. The responsibility for fighting the war fell on the shoulders of American combat troops. The American soldiers who arrived in Vietnam in the early stages of combat commitment brought with them the concept of 'truth, justice and the American way,' secure in the right and might of the United States. However, it was not long before the situation became less clear cut. Most young

Right: a sergeant of the US Army's 1st Infantry Division wades through a jungle stream during a search and destroy mission.

Inset right: American troops take cover in a trench dug by the Viet Cong during Operation Hawthorne in 1966.

American draftees were unprepared for the oriental society and suffered from culture shock. The only reference on which they could draw was the image of the Japanese as a devious, vicious enemy given by cinema.

Defining the enemy was another major dilemma. It was difficult to trust the South Vietnamese people but it was equally difficult to determine precisely where and who the enemy was. Although well trained in combat techniques, guerrilla warfare was alien to American combat troops. Even when the enemy was defined and located it was virtually impossible to force that enemy to stand and fight. The seemingly endless cycle of futile searching and tedious waiting soon frustrated and demoralized American soldiers. Added to that were the contradictory wartime policies of 'no fire zones' and 'free territories' in which American soldiers could not pursue or harass the enemy. Political interference in military ventures has proven to be counterproductive yet in Vietnam the United States and South Vietnamese governments persistantly interfered. These and other problems contributed to a 'who cares' attitude which permeated the ranks of combat and support personnel. As the war wound down in the early 1970s these problems were emphasized by the absurd establishment of a peacetime army atmosphere complete with crisply starched uniforms and 'spit shined' boots.

Other disruptive factors originated in the United States. The growing disillusionment of combat forces spread to that segment of American society most affected by the war, peers of soldiers. Whether potential draftees or intimates of those who served in Vietnam, they became increasingly active in antiwar demonstrations. In 1965 opinion polls indicated that 60 percent of Americans supported President Johnson's commitment of troops to Vietnam, 16 percent opposed it and 24 percent of the population lacked any opinion on the subject. However, between 1965 and 1966 American casualties in Southeast Asia rose from 1300–4800 confirmed deaths. The Tet Offensive of 1968 provoked a drastic shift in public opinion. Americans had believed McNamara's wartime statistics and his assurances that the North Vietnamese and the Viet Cong were incapacitated. Tet proved otherwise and the 'Big Lie' exponents gained support. This initiated another cycle of frustration and confusion in the ranks of combat troops. The growing antagonism in the United States was unjustly aimed toward Vietnam veterans and soldiers.

The civil rights movement in the United States had an impact in Vietnam. By 1968 black Americans had classified the conflict as a 'white-man's war.' Although black soldiers fought alongside white, were wounded and killed, and displayed heroism and self-sacrifice in Vietnam, racism and inequality continued within the army and on their return to the United States. Charges were being levied that white draftees more often received skilled training, which placed them in the relative safety of rear-echelon units, while black soldiers were destined for the front-lines.

There was an enormous difference between the American serviceman bound for Vietnam and his World War I and II predecessors. McNamara's corporate image approach had a widespread impact. The average age of combat troops in Vietnam was 19, compared to 26 in War II. Their transfer to and from Vietnam was a traumatic experience. In as little as 12 hours raw recruits were taken from a peacetime atmosphere to the midst of a war zone. World War I and II recruits took weeks, even months to reach their destinations and they left a country industrially mobilized and emotionally geared for war. Neither were Vietnam-bound soldiers sent in the camaraderie of units but as individuals to fill isolated slots in assembly-line fashion. The return from Vietnam was traumatic, with its rapid change from combat soldier to civilian without a transition period to assimilate and cope with the experiences the troops had encountered. Combined with other factors, this psychological shock resulted in a Post-Traumatic Stress disorder or Delayed Stress Syndrome. The essential need of persons who encounter cataclysmic events to discuss their situation with others of similar experience was denied the returning veteran by the means of his return and the lack of understanding of those who had not shared his experience. It is estimated that at least 60 percent of Vietnam combat veterans and a high percentage of women who served in support roles who survive in 1980 have some form of delayed stress disorder. Although this disorder is not a mental illness it manifests itself in higher divorce, suicide and criminal conviction rates than nonveteran peers. Successful methods of dealing with the Delayed Stress Syndrome are only being recognized now.

Yet another major difference between Vietnam veterans and their World War II counterparts is the high proportion of disabled men and women. Those who in previous wars would have lost their lives were saved by the rapid medical attention which the helicopter could provide, but they became permanently disabled. American prisoners of war suffered devastating trauma. Although there were some senseless postwar tragedies among prisoners of war, former prisoners need for counselling was eventually recognized.

The men who fought in Vietnam epitomize the chaos, disillusion and despair of a nation which was confronted with a situation it could not comprehend. The legacy of Vietnam must be accepted. The lessons learned must be applied to the future. The acceptance of and compassion for the men and women who served in Vietnam is the first step of the healing process. The self-confidence of the United States as a nation can not otherwise be restored.

9 THE FINAL COLLAPSE

In the wake of American military disengagement from the war the Communist factions tightened their grip in South Vietnam. By 1974 American financial aid had been reduced to less than $700,000,000, or less than three percent of the gross expenditure in Vietnam in 1967, and further reductions were expected. The extravagant military expenditures of the Vietnam era and Johnson's Great Society program were just beginning to take their toll on the American economy. It was inevitable when the Communists launched their final offensive, the 'Third War for Vietnam,' in December 1974 that the South would fall. Although less than two years earlier the United States had promised Thieu's government support in the event of a Communist takeover bid, the American public adamantly refused to permit further military involvement in Southeast Asia.

From December 1974 through March 1975 the

Communist offensive progressed. If isolated the ARVN fought well but when President Thieu ordered his forces to withdraw to the coastal plains and major cities their morale was broken. What was essentially the final confrontation between ARVN and Communist forces occurred in late March at Xuan Loc, 40 miles northeast of Saigon. After six days of bitter fighting this force collapsed, and with it the Republic of Vietnam. Panic swept the country. On 3 April the United States began to airlift American civilians and diplomatic personnel from Saigon. President Gerald Ford ordered 'Operation Baby Lift,' which employed cargo aircraft to evacuate children, primarily orphans and those of mixed American and South Vietnamese parentage. Several allied nations participated in this massive effort.

Below: refugees from the fall of Saigon aboard USS Hancock.

By 15 April there was complete chaos in South Vietnam but Congress refused to commit American combat troops to the area for any reason. On 22 April Saigon was encircled. President Thieu denounced America for abandoning South Vietnam in its hour of need and then promptly resigned and fled to the United States. By 29 April American cargo aircraft and a fleet of helicopters had evacuated 1373 American civilians, 1000 US marine security personnel and more than 6000 South Vietnamese civilians. On 1 May Saigon fell. All symbols of the South Vietnamese government were destroyed and the former capital was renamed Ho Chi Minh City. Twelve days later, in a misguided show of strength, the US merchant ship *Mayaguez* was seized off the coast of Cambodia. It was apparently believed that the United States would accept the insult meekly, but within 72 hours the merchant vessel's crew had been rescued, with a loss of 18 American lives. However the well-executed rescue took a second seat to the continuing media coverage of the events in Vietnam itself.

The ultimate collapse of South Vietnam was preordained. Nevertheless it sent shockwaves around the world and refocussed attention on Vietnam and the United States' role in Southeast Asia. The most important unanswered question was why, after all the time, money and lives expended, did Vietnam fall? One of the most important factors in the collapse of South Vietnam was the manner in which the United States channelled its energies in that country. The military effort was all important. The United States failed to create a stable, concerned South Vietnamese government. Fulfilling the needs of the civilian population was delegated to the various ineffectual regimes of South Vietnam. The United States made no real effort to win the hearts of the people.

However there were other, more tangible, reasons for the collapse. The failure of the Vietnamization program and the departure of American military support upset the military balance which had been maintained with the NVA/VC. The ARVN had become dependent on American combat, air and support expertise and technology. Although many of the sophisticated weapons systems and aircraft remained in Vietnam, ARVN forces were incapable of employing them to their full potential without American guidance. South Vietnam was surrounded by three Communist governments, North Vietnam, Laos and Cambodia. It was therefore isolated with no hope of support from any of its neighbors or former allies when the final offensive came. The loss of American strategic and tactical guidance in this situation resulted in disastrous mismanagement of the defense of the South. President Thieu ordered troop maneuvers with no understanding of deployment strategies. His 'no retreat' mandate prior to the final defeat of his army contributed more than any other factor to the disintegration of the morale of the

Above: a Marine guards evacuees from Saigon, April 1975.
Above right: US troops await airlift.

Army of the Republic of Viet Nam. The troops were obviously being sacrificed without hope of altering the outcome of the war.

The governments of South Vietnam were largely to blame for the conditions throughout their country which contributed to the collapse. The United States government was directly and indirectly responsible for this. Although billions of American dollars were sent to South Vietnam to initiate social programs and reforms, the United States turned a blind eye to the blatant greed and corruption which converted those funds into personal gain for high-ranking government officials. Little consideration was given to the long-term consequences of this attitude.

Finally, the notion was perpetrated that after the withdrawal of American troops in early 1973 the United States would, if necessary, return to aid South Vietnam militarily. It was a severe psychological blow to the ARVN and population of South

Vietnam when American combat forces departed. There had been no great love for the Americans but the South Vietnamese had grown accustomed to their presence. However, it was still believed that the United States would rescue South Vietnam from massive aggression by the North. The implications of the 1973 'Presidential War Powers Act' was not fully understood. In view of the antiwar sentiments there was little likelihood of Congress approving the reestablishment of combat troops in Vietnam. Such a move would have meant political suicide for its proponents. When America did not provide military support during the NVA/VC offensive, the South's morale was shattered.

The wisdom of ever sending troops to South Vietnam must be seriously questioned. America became involved through its desire to make a stand against Communism and, once begun, American military involvement in Southeast Asia was a vicious, self-perpetuating cycle. Yet the United States set no true value on South Vietnam. This was evidenced by the lack of concern for any but military objectives and by the desperation with which the Nixon Administration sought an 'honorable' means to extricate the United States. In the late 1960s the American people refused to countenance the continuation of the war and the nightmare truly began.

The final question which must be asked is whether or not the United States learned anything from the Vietnam experience. More than $150,000,000,000 was spent on the war. At least 50,000 service men and women died. More than 200,000 were permanently disabled. Considering MacNamara's policy of body counts, it is possible that these figures are grossly underestimated. The sacrifice of those who fought and died, and who fought and lived, can not be forgotten. Foreign-policy makers and the American people must remember to weigh the cost against the gain. Perhaps most importantly, the United States must learn from its intervention in Southeast Asia never to engage in a coalition war and simultaneously attempt to reform and transform the ally, never to expect unwavering support from confirmed allies, regardless of the 'right' of the venture, and that sophisticated technology is not sufficient in itself to produce victory. It is the determination and support of the people, of the United States and the ally, which determines victory.

Much remains to be done and undone in the wake of Vietnam but there is no simple answer or cure for the lingering effects of this colossal error in judgment. If Vietnam is not to be repeated American foreign policy must become consistent in its approach to other governments around the world. Vietnam should not be whitewashed or ignored but its lessons should form the foundation of a more realistic perspective on the role of the United States as a defender of freedom among the world super powers.

Acknowledgments
The author would like to thank:
Adrian Hodgkins the designer.
Penny Murphy, the indexer.
Richard Natkiel, who prepared the maps.

Picture Credits
Bison Picture Library: pp 6, 8, 10, 32, 39, 45,
53.
Maps © Richard Natkiel: pp 10, 11, 31.
USAF: pp 33, 36–37, 40–41, 48, 51, 54–55, 63.
US Army: pp 2–3, 4–5, 9, 12, 13, 14, 14–15, 16,
17, 18, 19, 22, 24, 25, 26, 28, 29, 30, 31, 34, 35,
37, 38, 42, 43, 44, 46, 47, 50, 56 (upper), 56–57,
59.
US Navy: pp 7, 20, 23, 56 (lower).
US Marines: pp 1, 27, 61, 62.